HOW TO DEVELOP CHILDREN AS RESEARCHERS

Mary Kellett is Director of the Children's Research Centre at the Open University and lectures in the Faculty of Education. She comes from a strong practitioner background having worked for several years as a teacher and a children's social worker. She has published on a wide range of issues including additional learning needs, disaffection, self-esteem, ethics and power relations.

How to Develop Children as Researchers

A Step-by-Step Guide to Teaching the Research Process

Mary Kellett

SAGE Publications

Los Angeles • London • New Delhi • Singapore

www.sagepublications.com

SAGE Publications Ltd
1 Oliver's Yard
55 City Road
London EC1Y 1SP

SAGE Publications Inc
2455 Teller Road
Thousand Oaks
California 91320

SAGE Publications India Pvt. Ltd
B 1/I 1 Mohan Cooperative Industrial Area
Mathura Road, New Delhi 110 044
India

SAGE Publications Asia-Pacific Pte Ltd
33 Pekin Street #02-01
Far East Square
Singapore 048763

Library of Congress Control Number 2004115431

A catalogue record for this book is available from the British Library

ISBN 978-1-4129-0829-0 (hbk)
ISBN 978-1-4129-0830-6 (pbk)

Typeset by Dorwyn, Wells, Somerset
Printed in Great Britain by Cpod, Trowbridge, Wiltshire
Printed on paper from sustainable resources

CONTENTS

ACKNOWLEDGEMENTS

My thanks to all the young researchers and colleagues I have worked with on this project. They are too many to name but their enthusiasm and support have helped make this book possible.

And

For my father, Denis, who continues to inspire us all.

*I*NTRODUCTION

Why Teach Research Methodology to Children?

In the adult world research process is greatly valued as an advanced learning tool and whetstone for critical thinking. The importance of research in professional and personal development is increasingly being acknowledged. So why should children not benefit in a similar way? Traditionally, children have been excluded from this learning process because research methodology is considered too difficult for them. Principal obstacles focus around three key barriers: age (and by implication, competence), knowledge and skills. If we can find ways to overcome these barriers and explore innovative approaches to engage children in the research process then we can access a rich –and, hitherto, largely untapped – source through which to develop creativity, critical thinking skills and analytical capability. The content of this book is the result of two years' pioneering research exploring, piloting and refining optimal ways to teach research methodology to children without compromising its core principles. The model expounded here seeks to distil rather than dilute the research process. It draws on both the author's research expertise and her classroom teaching experience in the design of an interactive teaching programme which children can meaningfully engage with.

Despite the many changes in the last decade, the National Curriculum is still regarded by many as over-prescriptive in content, broad brush in coverage and didactic in approach. A frequent complaint by educationalists is that, with the demise of topic work, children rarely have the opportunity to study something in real depth (Pyke, 1993). The 'project' still survives in many schools, albeit in a much diluted form, as typified by an 11-year-old child researcher who said: 'I used to think that doing projects meant gathering stuff from books and the internet. Projects are more than "cut things out and stick things in". Active research offers an ideal opportunity for pupils to engage with a subject in great depth and work with primary, self-generated data.

The research process also provides a good vehicle for metacognition and critical thinking, both through the appraisal of other people's research and in the design of a pupil's own research study. The ability to funnel down to a focused research question, and, where appropriate, testable hypotheses, is a

1

prized skill which can be transferred to many other areas of the curriculum. Choosing an appropriate methodology to answer research question(s) extends children's logical and lateral thinking and requires the application and/or adaptation of learned knowledge. The process of collecting data frequently requires the handling of large amounts of information – much larger than pupils are normally required to work with in the classroom – and the successful manipulation of these quantities of data develops pupils' organisational and management skills, crucial elements of good study skills.

Pilot work (Kellett et al., 2004) showed that it is the data analysis stage of research where pupils take great strides in their learning. The close scrutiny required to deconstruct layer upon layer of observations from data and the further skills required to compare and contrast within and across these sets of data significantly develops higher-order thinking.

Disseminating the findings from a research study sharpens writing, communication and organizational skills. However, something less tangible and not as easily measured has been shown to be an equally beneficial outcome –the enhanced learning that occurs through *motivation* and *ownership*. There are many examples in the literature of arrested learning and challenging behaviour resulting from disaffection, demotivation or a misalignment between learning and teaching style (Pollard and Bourne, 1994). We recognise that there are far too many disaffected pupils, some of them highly able, who are falling through the learning net. Such pupils are more likely to be motivated by the prospect of working on a topic of their own choosing which interests them, which they can initiate and drive themselves and take ownership of. There are significant implications for the positive effect this has on learner self-esteem (Lawrence, 1988).

A further justification for the teaching of research process to children is the creation of knowledge. Learning is about acquiring, understanding and applying knowledge but it is also about using those skills to *create* knowledge. Pupils rarely get an opportunity to create their own original knowledge in schools. A vast amount of new knowledge is generated by research and much knowledge is also affirmed or discredited by research. One of these bodies of knowledge is about children and childhood, yet it has been constructed almost exclusively by adults. In the wake of the United Nations *Convention on the Rights of the Child* (1989) and the changing perspectives on child status, this is no longer a tenable state of affairs. Children are acknowledged as experts on their own lives (Alderson, 2000; Mayall, 2000; Christensen and Prout 2002) and if adults genuinely want to understand children and childhood, better ways to seek out child perspective and unlock child voice must be sought. One initiative has been the increased involvement of children as participant and co-researchers (e.g. Johnson et al., 1998; Nieuwenhuys, 2001; Jones et al., 2002) and there is a growing body of literature on the role of children and young people as researchers (Boyden and Ennew, 1997; Alderson, 2000: Fielding, 2004). But participatory research of this kind is still adult designed, adult led, and conceived from an adult perspective. Very rarely do adults hand over the reins to children to initiate and drive their own research. Indeed, in many instances adult-led research about children is undertaken in power-laden settings with captive child audiences –such as schools. Questions have to be asked about the validity of child research (and the knowledge it generates) in contexts where adults control children's time, occupation of space, choice of clothing, times of eating –even their mode of social interaction.

It would be naive to imagine that even the most accomplished ethnographers could entirely rid themselves of adult baggage and become children again (Thorne, 1993). It would appear, therefore, that the key to a better understanding of children and childhood is children themselves – as active researchers. Children ask different questions, have different priorities and concerns and see the world through different eyes. This important contribution to knowledge can only be made by children themselves. However, children lack the skills and training to be able to undertake their own research. So we have come full circle, back to the central question –why not teach them? –and have arrived at precisely what this book is all about: a step-by-step guide to teaching children to become active researchers. Extensive pilot work has shown that it is possible to do this with most children aged 12 to 14 years and that the approach is accessible for gifted and talented children as young as 9 and 10. The quality of work of such young children has already been verified and welcomed by the adult research community (Kellett et al., 2004) by the media (*Times Educational Supplement*, 7th November 2003; BBC Radio 4, *The Learning Curve*, 25th November 2003; *Guardian*, 24th March 2004) and by practising teachers (Research in Practice conference, Westminster Institute of Education, 2003; Spotlight on Learning conference, National Union of Teachers, 2004).

How this Book is Organised

This book is designed for use with pupils aged 10 to 14 years. It is suitable for gifted and talented pupils in Years 5 and 6 through to pupils of average ability in Year 9, and includes differentiated activities so that teachers can adapt the content for their pupils. The teaching in each chapter is presented in an accessible way, distilling much of the complexities of the research process for novice readers. It is possible, therefore, that able pupils and those in the older age range could work with much of this book in the style of a textbook. The book is divided into four parts: The Nature of Research; Data Collection; Data Analysis and Dissemination. Part I is more theoretical than other parts and teachers should feel free to intersperse this with some of the more skill-based teaching in Part II (Data Collection) rather than necessarily running the programme in strict sequence. It is not advisable, however, to introduce any Part III teaching (Data Analysis) until Parts I and II have been covered.

It is important to establish that doing research is not an activity confined to able pupils. By adjusting the support provided, diverse groups of children can also be empowered to undertake research. Groups of children with a specific identity such as disabled children, children from minority ethnic groups, 'looked-after' children or children with learning difficulties all have unique contributions to make to our knowledge and understanding, and are to be warmly encouraged as active researchers.

Each chapter contains a summary of learning outcomes, timed teaching content and a core activity which has been specially designed to distil the teaching content and engage pupils with the main learning objectives. This core activity is aimed at the middle age range (able 11-12-year-olds) but should be equally suitable for highly able 9-10-year-olds or 13-14-year-olds of average ability. It is presented at an intermediate level with suggestions given on how to differentiate the activity for different ages and abilities. For ease of use the core materials are reproduced in a photocopiable format and appear in the Photocopiable Resource Bank at the end of the book. Key research terms for each chapter appear in a highlighted box with accompanying definitions and build up to form a comprehensive glossary which is reproduced in full at the end of the book. These key research terms also form the basis of a series of card games known as Expert Researcher card games. Beginning with only a few definitions, the card games are relatively simple but become increasingly complex as more terms are added and new games are introduced.

The teaching programme is made up of 12 sessions each lasting about 90 minutes plus 20-60 minutes of follow-up work. These timings are approximate and will vary according to the age and ability of the pupils concerned. They have been calculated from pilot work with able 10-12-year-olds. The programme lends itself to wholesale adoption should teachers want to start a school Research Club, focus on research as a discrete study or use the programme as a gifted and talented initiative. Alternatively, elements of it can be incorporated into Personal, Social and Health Education (PSHE), Citizenship, Literacy, Science and other appropriate areas of the curriculum.

The Children's Research Centre, based at the Open University campus in Milton Keynes, UK, provides a focal point for the development of children and young people as active researchers. It offers comprehensive training workshops for teachers and practitioners, regular conferences, a learning community, a supportive network and outreach programmes. Visit the website http://childrens-research-centre.open.ac.uk for more information.

PART I

The Nature of Research

What is Research?

Learning aims	Knowledge content	Skills	Interactive elements	Pupil follow-up work	Curriculum links
Begin to develop an understanding of the nature of research	The nature of research	Critical thinking	Group discussion	Read and reflect on a short research paper	Literacy
	The nature of enquiry	Separating fact and opinion	Expert Researcher card games		Science
Begin to have an appreciation of ethical issues in research	The importance of research	Interpreting research findings			
	Different types of research and their main characteristics				

TEACHING CONTENT FOR SESSION 1

Timing: 90 minutes + 30 minutes follow-up work.

The Nature of Research

Research is all around us, indeed, it feels at times as if we cannot escape it! Newspapers are saturated with articles beginning 'Research findings show ...' and go on to inform us about the UK having the highest number of teenage pregnancies in Europe or that a given percentage of under-12s are obese. Out shopping, we are accosted by 'researchers' wanting to know what our preferred brand of shampoo is or whether we think the Prime Minister should step down from office. At school, teachers might ask pupils to 'research' the medicinal plants of the rainforest or the religious practices of the Aztecs. On television we are introduced to documentaries that chart the findings of the latest breakthrough in cancer research or the cloning of human embryos. Can all of these be research? If so, what *is* research?

One way of answering these questions is to explain that 'research' is a generic term covering a vast and diverse range of activities. The term is also sometimes used quite loosely to refer to a process of enquiry. One of the characteristics which these activities all have in common is that they seek to 'find out'. Research is essentially about 'finding out' by collecting data. But what distinguishes 'research' from a 'finding-out activity' is that it also needs to be *ethical, sceptical* and *systematic* (Robson, 2002) and, in however small a way, seeks to make a difference. Other finding-out activities may have some, but not all, of these characteristics and may even be unethical –for example, some finding-out activities may be based on criminal activity or rely on deception.

Most pupils, at some point, undertake a school project. Typically this will involve finding out information about a particular topic from books, libraries and the Internet. This is a worthwhile learning experience but a research study, in the sense of our earlier description, goes much further and additionally requires:

- the formulation of a research question and possibly testable hypotheses
- a methodological design
- the collection of raw data
- in-depth analysis
- a scrutiny of validity
- the generation of new knowledge.

Why is Research Important?

It is not unreasonable to question whether we should be undertaking research at all. Some research can be very expensive, so we need to be persuaded that it is an important activity. Some benefits from research are more tangible than others –for example, research that might find a drug to cure multiple sclerosis or slow the onset of Alzheimer's disease would be universally welcomed. Other kinds of research such as those that investigate our relationship with, and place in, the social world might appear less easy to justify but they are important, too, because they increase our knowledge and understanding. This brings us to a crucial aspect of research which is often overlooked –the generation of new knowledge.

Research is important because:

- its innovative and exploratory character can bring about beneficial change (e.g. cures for debilitating diseases)

- its sceptical enquiry can result in poor or unethical practices being questioned (e.g. corporal punishment in schools)

- its rigorous and systematic nature extends knowledge and promotes problem-solving (e.g. extending our knowledge about different types of nutrition can help promote problem-solving with regard to healthy living).

Research and 'Truth'

Truth is not an absolute, just as certainty can never be an absolute. We all experience the world in different ways. We have different perspectives and different experiences, and we do not always agree about what is true in those different experiences. So how can we establish 'truth' when we are faced with different, and sometimes even conflicting, experiences? Rather than thinking about research in terms of establishing 'truth' I prefer to think in terms of research establishing 'knowledge and understanding', where 'truth' is related to the honesty, rigour and reliability of the approach.

So, what research sets out to do is to establish the 'truth' of something through a systematic and rigorous process of critical enquiry where even the most commonplace assumption is not readily accepted until it has been validated. Kerlinger (1986) refers to this sceptical form of enquiry as checking subjective belief against objective reality. Furthermore any 'truth' established by research also has a self-correcting process at work in the ongoing public scrutiny to which it is subjected (Cohen et al., 2000) and any research inaccuracies will ultimately be discovered and either corrected or discarded. Short of the absolute truth which we have established is not possible, good research comes very close. It uses an approach which combines reasoning and experience and has built-in mechanisms to protect against error, bias and subjectivity. Borg (1963) regarded research as the most successful approach to the discovery of truth.

Research and Ethics

We will be examining ethics in more detail at various stages later in the book but it is important to introduce the concept of ethics at the outset as this is an essential element of the research process. Research activity has to be ethical, to have regard for the interests and needs of participants involved and also those upon whom the findings of research might have an impact. Research must not cause harm or distress to any individual. When doing research we have to be frank, open and critical about what, how and why our research is taking place. Researchers have a duty to make observations accurately and clearly, whether or not such observations agree with their hypotheses or any previous assumptions. Therefore, researchers do not just 'make an observation' or 'take a measurement', they must also describe the circumstances in which that observation or measurement is made and who is making it. Researchers expect their methods as well as their findings to be open to public scrutiny. This concern to be *systematic*, *sceptical* and *ethical* is what distinguishes empirical research from other types of finding out activity such as that undertaken by barristers or journalists where investigative findings are used to advocate a particular view, creating evidence and argument to support that view rather than engaging in any doubt or looking for any evidence that might challenge that view. This does not mean that the view is necessarily false but it may mean that individuals such as barristers or journalists fail to acknowledge when it might be.

BOX 1.1 KEY RESEARCH TERMS FOR SESSION 1

data: information (which can be numerical or descriptive) which are analysed and used as the basis for making decisions in research. Data is plural, the singular form is *datum* but it is unusual to only ever have one piece of information in research so the word datum rarely appears in research writing.

ethical: making sure that the well-being, interests and concerns of those involved in research are looked after. It is imperative that research does not cause harm or distress to any of the participants at any time. These days research is generally expected to follow a code of ethics laid down by an authoritative body.

sceptical: being prepared to question or doubt the nature of findings – even the most commonplace. The process of doubting is an important stage in research if we are to acquire relative certainty (we can never have absolute certainty). So, a sceptical approach tries to find things out but also looks for counter arguments which might reject as well as confirm the findings. Furthermore, researchers allow their findings to be scrutinised by other people and expect them to try and disprove the findings.

systematic: researchers think about what they are going to do and how and why they are doing it in a methodical, purposeful, step-by-step way. Everything is set out very explicitly, e.g. if a researcher is going to 'find out' by observation then exactly what is to be observed, who is doing the observing, how, where, in what circumstances and for how long, has to be made clear.

Core Activity

This activity can be done either as a discussion group or as a written exercise (or both) and suggestions for differentiation are given. It appears in a convenient photocopiable format (Photocopiable Resource 1) at the end of the book.

Intermediate level

The core activity draws together the main teaching threads of Session 1 by addressing a frequently posed question about the difference between a researcher and a journalist. Both researchers and journalists engage in finding out activities but as has been explained earlier, one of the principal differences is the *sceptical* nature of empirical research compared to journalism. A journalist's report will have a theme or angle and data are often selected to fit this theme, commonly either ignoring, or failing to search for, any data which might disconfirm this theme or angle. Good research might begin by posing a similar question to a journalist but has to be open-minded to possible findings and not only examines the data from a variety of perspectives but also analyses the circumstances in which the data are collected because this could have an important bearing on the findings.

Pupils read the following report (fictionally constructed for the purpose of this activity) and consider whether it is 'valid research'. Some think prompts are given.

UK fast-food diet producing 'fat' babies

New statistics out this month suggest that our obsession with fast food is now producing fat babies. This year a record number of babies –103 –have weighed in at more than 12lb 12 oz. According to figures from the Office for National Statistics, 1.68% of babies weighed more than 10lb this year compared with 1.45% ten years ago. Boy babies weigh an average of 7lb 8oz, a rise of 2oz from 1973. Experts state that babies who are padded with fat all over their bodies –including, in some cases, their skulls –have a greater tendency towards obesity. In Japan where fast food is not as popular and the average diet includes an abundance of raw fish the average birth weight is 6lb 10oz and in India the average birth weight is less than 6lb.

- Is this report 'research'?
- Would you describe it as systematic, sceptical and ethical?

- What other information would researchers need before they could draw the same conclusions as this journalist?
- How differently do you think a research report might be constructed?

Guided comment

There are several reasons why a report like this should not be regarded as valid research. Yes, some genuine data are being cited (from the Office for National Statistics) but only selected pieces of data are being used so it is not a systematic approach. It is not sceptical because it does not also look for data that might disconfirm the claim it is making. Moreover, the style of reporting is unethical because it suggests a link between heavier babies and bad dietary habits without providing any evidence to support this assertion. We are not told, for example, how the reporter knows that the mothers of the 103 babies born heavier than 12lb 12oz ate a diet of fast food. This appears to be just an assumption on the part of the reporter probably based on a common perception that we are a nation addicted to fast food.

A great deal more data would be required before a researcher could reach the conclusion drawn by this journalist. Birth weight is linked to many factors other than diet. Researchers would want to know the height and weight of the parents of each of these heavy babies. They would need precise information about the dietary habits of the mothers. They would want to know if there were any other conditions that affect birth weight, e.g. whether the mothers were smokers or had medical conditions such as diabetes. Before they could reach a conclusion about whether babies are genuinely heavier than they were ten years ago researchers would also need data about all of these factors (i.e. weight and height of parents, diet of mothers, etc.) from ten years ago. The report states that 1.68 per cent of babies weigh more than 10lb compared with 1.45 per cent ten years ago, but if parents, on average, also weigh 1.68 per cent more than they did ten years ago then babies are only getting heavier in absolute terms, not in relative terms. Indeed, if statistics were to show that parents, on average, weigh 2.5 per cent more than they did ten years ago then in *relative* terms babies are *actually getting less heavy*. If statistics did confirm an average increase in adult weight, researchers would need to know what conditions might account for this. One reason could be diet, or different levels of exercise, but it might also be due to increased height. This would lead them off on another trail to check out the differences in average heights of adult males and females over the last ten years. This kind of 'finding out trail' where one question leads to another and therefore to another new search for information commonly characterises research activity. Indeed, research enquiry can lead to new questions being asked which might not otherwise have been thought of.

The report also compares average birth weights in the UK, Japan and India –but without giving any information on average adult weight in these other countries. A comparison is being made on insufficient information and can lead to false conclusions. The smaller birth weights in Japan might be linked to diet, but they might also be linked to other factors, e.g. whether the average Japanese person is smaller than the average British person. The same logic applies to the conclusion implied about Indian people.

Juxtaposing some genuine facts (e.g. the data from the Office for National Statistics) alongside speculative comment (e.g. UK mothers eat fast food) is sometimes used by journalists to give an element of credibility to their reports which then lends credibility to their non-empirical claims. This can be misleading for the reader and the pressure for sensation-grabbing headlines can, on occasions, produce damaging reports. This is not to say that all media reports lack validity or are unethical; there are some very responsible journalists who provide important information and valuable insights.

Differentiating the core activity

The core activity lends itself to small group discussion and/or a written critique exercise. It can be adapted according to the ability of the pupils you are working with.

Simpler level

Invite pupils to highlight facts in one colour and opinion/speculation in another and then discuss the overall balance between fact and opinion in the article.

Advanced level

(This advanced level activity will require longer than the 90 minutes allocated for Session 1 and this should be taken into account when planning the timing of the session and/or the follow-up work.) Provide pupils with statistical data about adult heights and weights from the current year and from a decade ago and then ask them to critique the article in the light of this additional information. Alternatively, a blank table (see Table 1.1) could be provided and pupils asked to find this information out for themselves from an Internet search.

Table 1.1 Example of a blank template for an Internet data search

Country	Average female height		Average female weight		Average male height		Average male weight		Average baby weight	
	1994	2004	1994	2004	1994	2004	1994	2004	1994	2004
USA										
UK										
Japan										
India										
Sweden										

Expert Researcher Card Games

Over the period of the 12 teaching sessions featured in this book, pupils are invited to play the Expert Researcher card games. These help build up familiarity with, and understanding of, key research vocabulary. At the end of Session 1 the games are relatively easy because there are only four key research terms involved. However, new terms are added each session and by the time pupils reach Session 12 the games become quite complex and demanding and pupils become increasingly familiar with the key research terms. As the Expert Researcher card games will be used throughout the programme it is worthwhile laminating these cards and making them as attractive as possible. It is also useful to make several sets so that pupils can play alone, in pairs or in small groups.

Write each of the four key research terms (those that appear in Box 1.1) onto four blank playing cards. Then, on four separate playing cards write the definition of each key word (copy this from the wording given in Box 1.1). The first card game is a simple familiarisation game and older/more able pupils may prefer to skip this one.

Game 1: 'Match up'

Shuffle the two sets of cards together and then place them face down in a pile on a table. In turn, players take a card from the pile and read it aloud. If this is a key research term card they attempt a definition, if it is a definition card they attempt to name the key research term it refers to. They then return the card to the bottom of the pile and continue the game until players can confidently match a key research term with its correct definition. Once they can do this any of the games described in subsequent chapters (a new game is introduced at the end of each teaching session) can be played. Even better, pupils can be encouraged to devise their own games with the cards.

Follow-up Work

To embed some of the core principles learned from Session 1 and to begin to sharpen critical thinking skills, pupils are encouraged to read a short research paper on a child-oriented topic and reflect on three or four elements (predetermined by the teacher) of the paper so that they can contribute to a group discussion at the start of Session 2. A suggestion is given below of a research paper which has been used successfully in this way with able pupils from Year 5 upwards. This is only one example and teachers may well have their own ideas for other suitable material to use.

Suggested research paper for this task

Leonard, M. (2002) Working on your doorstep: child newspaper deliverers in Belfast, *Childhood*, 9(2): 190–204.

Suggested questions for a focused discussion on this research paper

1 The author discusses the skills needed to be a newspaper deliverer. Do you think these skills are undervalued by the general public?

2 What are your views on the law relating to child employment as described by the author of the paper?

3 What do you think about the health and safety issues related to being a newspaper deliverer?

4 Do you think newspaper deliverers are exploited?

Key Reflection from Session 1

Research is about asking questions, exploring issues and reflecting on findings. It is concerned with extending knowledge, pursuing 'truth' and must always be ethical.

Suggested Further Reading

Fraser, S., Lewis, V., Ding, S., Kellett, M. and Robinson, C. (eds) (2004) *Doing Research with Children and Young People*, London: Sage in association with OUP.

This is an edited collection of chapters written around a range of issues relating to research with children and young people.

CHAPTER 2

Learning from Other People's Research

Learning aims	Knowledge content	Skills	Interactive elements	Pupil follow-up work	Curriculum links
Begin to have an appreciation of good and poor research	The nature of research	Skim reading	Group discussion	Read and reflect on a short research paper	Literacy
	Access to and orientation of research studies	Content sifting	Expert Researcher card games		
Understand the way a research paper is structured		Critical reading			
Access higher order reading skills					

TEACHING CONTENT FOR SESSION 2

Timing: 90 minutes + 30 minutes follow-up task.

Before the start of this session, have a short discussion about the research paper pupils read for the follow-up task.

Different Types of Research

There are many different types of research and they are categorised in varying ways by different writers. Whole books have been devoted to this issue, but for our purposes I shall attempt to simplify the principal debates and summarise the main categories of research.

Broadly speaking research can be divided into two categories: positivist and naturalistic. Positivist research is often described as having a scientific method and is concerned with objectivity and controllability, with the ability to predict and measure and with cause and effect. Knowledge about the world is generated by understanding these causal links. Furthermore, any knowledge generated must be able to be validated empirically (from within our practical experience). A common form of positivist research is known as the experimental design because it frequently seeks answers to a research question by setting up an experiment. This is done by the control and manipulation of what we call *variables*. In a pure experimental design a researcher wants to isolate a variable so that its effect can be measured or tested. We will be learning more about experimental research in Chapter 5.

Naturalistic research is concerned with *exploring* the nature of things rather than testing hypotheses about them. It focuses on understanding and interpreting the world in terms of the people in that world, maintaining that the social world can only be understood by individuals who are part of that world. Therefore enquiry cannot be 'external' or 'objective' as in the scientific model but has to be done from the 'inside' and is coloured by individual experience. This makes the research more subjective and open to interpretation. A common form of naturalistic research is ethnography. The word ethnography derives from two words 'ethno' meaning people and 'graphy' meaning a description of something. So, ethnographic research is about describing people. To be able to do this an ethnographer has to become a participant observer and experience what it is like for the people who live in their cultural world. We sometimes talk about ethnographers 'immersing' themselves for long periods of time – sometimes several years – in order to explore and understand the people whom they are studying.

Quantitative research provides information about the world in the form of numbers. This involves *measurement*. In quantitative research, measurement is a process that turns data into numbers by assigning a numerical value to things, events or people. There are two types of operation which produce numbers: counting and scaling. Counting is something we do every day and we can easily understand. Scaling refers to creating a continuum ranging from a very little of something to a great deal of something, e.g. a percentage scale ranges from 0 to 100 where 2 would be a very little and 96 would be a great deal. An agreement scale ranging from strongly agree to strongly disagree with several degrees of relative agreement/disagreement in between is an example of a quantifiable scale which can be used to test people's attitudes. Scaling enables us to compare things (or people or events) in a standardised way.

Qualitative research provides information about the world in non-numerical form, in other words in a *descriptive* way. This can take many forms such as oral accounts, photos or artefacts although the most common is qualitative data expressed as descriptions in words. Because of its more subjective nature, qualitative researchers frequently collect data from several sources. There are many qualitative techniques for collecting data but in this book, we will focus only on two: observation and interview. Qualitative approaches are generally considered to be less structured than quantitative approaches, indeed some models have virtually no structure at all at the point where the data are collected and it is only when the analysis begins that any kind of structure can be identified.

There is a long-standing debate concerning the differences and relative values of quantitative and qualitative research. In this book I make no value judgements about either approach. It is more important that the most *appropriate* method is chosen for a particular research study irrespective of whether this is a quantitative or qualitative approach. It is becoming increasingly common for research designs to incorporate elements of both quantitative and qualitative approaches.

BOX 2.1 KEY RESEARCH TERMS FOR SESSION 2

empirical: relates to something in our practical experience, derived from observation or experiment. It is linked to the idea that true knowledge is to be found within our practical experience rather than from speculative notions or ideas.

ethnography: the description of a culture or a way of life through a process of 'immersion' as a participant observer in that cultural world.

naturalistic: an approach that focuses on exploring the nature of things rather than testing hypotheses about them, on understanding and interpreting the world in terms of the people in that world. The world can only be understood by people who are part of that world and enquiry is consequently coloured by their individual experiences.

positivist: a scientific approach concerned with cause and effect, objectivity and controllability and with the ability to predict and measure. Knowledge about the world is generated by understanding these causal links.

qualitative: an approach which gathers data in a non-numerical (descriptive) form.

quantitative: an approach which gathers data in a quantifiable (numerical) form.

Learning from Other People's Research

There are vast numbers of research studies in the public domain, how do we judge what is good and poor research? Researchers are understandably keen to share the findings of their studies and to have their work accepted as a valid contribution to knowledge. If you remember from Session 1 we talked about researchers wanting to feel, in however small a way, that their findings 'make a difference'. Making a difference is not always about ground-breaking discoveries that bring us a cure for cancer or discover how to map human genes, making a difference is also about contributing to knowledge. Because we constantly question knowledge it is important that we continue to do research in areas where we already have knowledge as well as doing research in new, exploratory areas. Thus, some research studies merely confirm what has already been found out by someone else. This may be necessary because a previous research study might only have been on a small scale, for example, and it might be important to discover if the findings are valid on a larger scale or in different circumstances. This kind of research is sometimes called a replication study or, depending on how different the new circumstances are it might be regarded as an adaptation study. Some research studies disconfirm previous findings and this is an equally important part of the research process. If research was never questioned, disconfirmed or, on occasions, discredited, then knowledge would become stagnant and we would probably still believe the earth was flat! Other studies build on the findings of previous research and extend knowledge already created in that area.

If research sets out to 'make a difference' then there has to be a means whereby the findings can be shared with others, particularly with others who will benefit from any new knowledge which has been created. This is what we call dissemination. Dissemination is a process of spreading and sharing information. In research this means disseminating the findings, conclusions and reflections of the researcher(s). Often, this is done in the form of a research paper. This is a written report setting out what the study aimed to find out, the reasons why the study was undertaken, the methods used, what the findings were and a discussion of the implications of those findings. Papers which appear in academic journals normally have to go through a rigorous process of peer review, whereby other academics scrutinise the validity and ethics of the study in question, and decide whether it merits inclusion in a particular journal. This system is not perfect and occasionally good research is rejected and poor research published, but in the main it provides a robust platform on which bodies of knowledge are created.

Academic journals are only one outlet for research. Some studies are written up as books, others as articles in newspapers and some as reports which are circulated to colleagues. Much research is disseminated electronically through Internet websites and many academic journals are available in electronic format. Not all dissemination is in written form; some studies use the genre of video documentary. It is also common for research studies to be disseminated via oral presentation, generally at conferences held at local, national and international venues. This vast accumulation of research studies provides an essential 'body' of knowledge which helps us better understand the world we live in.

When researchers want to carry out a new study, they first look at this body of knowledge to find out what is already known in their field of interest. For example, if researchers were interested in exploring children's views about pay and working conditions for newspaper delivery they would first want to determine what had already been found out about young children in the labour market and critically appraise how relevant these findings are to the new researchers' intended question. It may be that some studies are quite old or do not relate to the age of child which the new researchers are interested in, or perhaps do not reflect a child perspective; nevertheless all will have points to argue and defend. There will frequently be disagreements between researchers. It is the task of the new researchers to critically review other studies, assess where their own particular question fits into the overall picture and decide whether there are any gaps in the knowledge currently held.

In order to be able to critically review other people's research we need to understand how to find our way around a reported study and what to look for. In the next part of this chapter we embark on a step-by-step orientation tour of a typical research paper, beginning with the title.

Finding your Way Around a Research Paper

The title

Titles are very important and when pupils come to write up their own research they will need to give this some careful thought. A good title should reflect the content of a research paper and give enough information to enable readers to decide whether or not it is relevant to their topic area and the particular research question they have in mind. Most research studies are catalogued on electronic databases and their titles can be searched via key words so it is even more important that titles contain key words which will assist dissemination. Titles are frequently in two parts, the first part might be a headline-grabbing phrase and the second a more perfunctory description of the study, e.g. 'Just teach us the skills please, we'll do the rest': empowering ten-year-olds as active researchers. The title of the research paper by Madeleine Leonard which was suggested for the follow-up task at the end of Chapter 1 has a similar format, i.e. Working on your doorstep: child newspaper deliverers in Belfast.

The abstract

Most research papers have an abstract which appears after the title and before the main body of the article. This is essentially a short summary of the research paper. It commonly gives some background and rationale for the study, describes the approach taken, outlines the main findings and indicates the principal conclusions drawn. Research reports are commonly structured in four sections – introduction, methodology, findings and discussion – and a good rule of thumb is that an abstract will provide a couple of sentences on each of these four parts.

References

Every research paper has a list of references at the end. Sometimes this is quite extensive. Throughout a paper, researchers refer to work that other people have done. They do this to set up a framework of existing knowledge in which to situate their own study. An important part of this process is critically reviewing how well previous research has addressed their topic and what the main theoretical views are. It may be that there are gaps in our knowledge about the topic or that some of this knowledge has been discredited or that new circumstances give rise to fresh questions being asked. Because most of the studies cited are usually in a written, published format this process is generally called a *literature review*. It would become quite cumbersome if, every time a research study is mentioned, the full reference of that work is given in the body of the text, especially if the same study is cited several times. Instead, a list of references is provided at the end of the research paper and referred to in the body of the text only by the surname of the author(s) and the date the work was written. When fully referenced, these must include:

- surname(s) and initials of author(s)
- date of publication
- full title
- if the work is from a journal article then the name of that journal, plus the volume, issue number (most journal have several issues within the same year) and page numbers
- if the work appears as a chapter in a book, then the full title of the book and editor(s) must be given
- place of publication
- name of publisher.

Here is an example of a reference to a journal article:

Woodhead, M. (1999) Combatting child labour: listen to what the children say, *Childhood*, 6(1): 27-49.

Woodhead is the surname of the author, M. is his initial. The article was written in 1999. Its title is 'Combatting child labour: listen to what the children say'. It can be found on pages 27-49 in volume 6, issue 1 of the journal, *Childhood*.

Here is an example of a reference to a book:

Christensen, P. and James, A. (eds) (2001) *Research with Children: Perspectives and Practices*, London: RoutledgeFalmer.

Christensen and James are the editors of the book titled *Research with Children: Perspectives and Practices*, which was published in 2001 by RoutledgeFalmer in London.

The introduction

An introduction to a paper sets out reasons why the researcher is interested in the particular topic and a rationale for why the research is being undertaken. It usually includes a section that critically appraises research studies already undertaken by other people in that field and identifies if there are any gaps in this body of knowledge. An introduction also sets out the particular question(s) which the study is going to explore.

The methodology

The method section is a crucial part of a research paper. It must give sufficient information so that a study can be repeated by someone else wanting to establish if the method produces similar findings. It also needs to give enough information so that readers can judge the merits of the study. The methods used have to be sound and appropriate for the research question otherwise the findings may not be valid. For example, if researchers want to investigate boys' and girls' attitudes to school lunchtime supervisors, one of the methods they might use is a questionnaire. It may be that the questionnaire elicits some useful data which is informative about gender attitudes to lunchtime supervisors. However, to be able to draw valid conclusions from the questionnaire findings they would need to have a similar number of responses from each gender. Supposing one of their questions was: *If someone is being unkind to you in the playground would you rather talk to the lunchtime supervisor about it or a teacher?* They analyse 134 completed questionnaires and draw the conclusion that 100 per cent of girls would rather talk to the lunchtime supervisor than their teacher compared to only 48 per cent of boys. However, if their sample of 134 is made up of 14 girls and 120 boys then their conclusion is clearly not a reliable one. The methodology section should provide a comprehensive description of all the circumstances involved in a research project, including all the ethical dimensions.

The findings

The findings of a study come from the data and these can be numerical or descriptive, or both. They address the research questions which have been asked and need to be presented clearly, succinctly and in a logical fashion. Often, numerical data are presented in tables or graphs so that the content is more easily assimilated by the reader. Some researchers analyse their findings as they present them, others reserve their analysis for the discussion section.

The discussion

This is the part of the paper where researchers analyse and discuss their findings in relation to what can be learned from the results, what the implications are, how this knowledge can further our understanding and how it fits into the context of other people's research in the chosen field.

Conclusion

This draws together the main findings which have been explored in the discussion section. It is intended to summarise the main points rather than make new ones.

One of the best ways to learn about research is to read other people's research papers. Encourage pupils to have a look at some journal articles and see if they can identify the characteristics listed above. Two excellent journals which feature articles about issues relating to children and childhood are *Childhood*, published by Sage and *Children & Society*, the journal of the National Children's Bureau, published by Wiley and Sons. They are available electronically, by subscription, and in most university libraries. Currently there is very little published research by children but several studies are featured on the website of the Children's Research Centre: http://childrens-research-centre.open.ac.uk.

Reviewing the literature will help pupils to:

- understand what other research already exists in their field of interest
- broaden their perspective
- give them new ideas
- set their topic in context
- develop their critical evaluation skills so that they can better critique their own and others' work
- spot gaps that have not been researched
- find studies that support and legitimate their argument.

Developing Advanced Reading Skills

Researchers develop their own ways of reviewing the literature. But two skills are crucial, however you approach the task. The first is to develop ways of deciding quickly whether or not a research paper is relevant. The second is to develop a critical approach to what you read.

Rapid reading

There are several ways in which pupils can speed up the literature-searching process. Skim reading is a skill we use when we want to find out very quickly if a research study is likely to be of interest without having to read everything word for word. If we are browsing the shelves of a library or a book shop for a new book to read we might pick one up and look at the title first and then turn the book over and read what is written about it on the blurb of the jacket cover. If it begins to interest us, we might look at the contents list or flick though a few pages to see how hard the language is and whether we think we like the author's style. Searching research literature uses some of these strategies to 'sift' the material and get to the gist of the argument. Here are some pointers for pupils.

- Look at the title. Does it contain any keywords that link to your topic?
- If the literature source is an article, read the abstract as this gives you a short summary of what the research is about.

- What year was it written? The research might be very old and out of date.

- Look at the subheadings in the article. Do they deal with subjects that are relevant to your topic?

- Read the first and last sentences in paragraphs and subsections because sometimes these are mini introductions and summaries of the section content.

- If you are looking at a book, read the first and last paragraphs of chapters as these will similarly reveal useful introductions to and summaries of the content.

Critical reading

The rapid reading skills outlined above will help sort the wheat from the chaff, but once pupils find a research paper which looks as though it is going to be a key source for their literature review they need to read the paper thoroughly and in a *critical way*. This means going beyond what the text is saying in order to assess its merit. They need to *analyse* and *evaluate* the rationale for the argument, weigh up the evidence and look for possible flaws in the method. For example, is the author making unfounded assumptions or claiming unwarranted conclusions? Is there another way to account for the findings that might have been overlooked?

Useful questions to ask when *analysing* a research paper are:

- What is the author trying to get me to accept?

- What evidence is the author providing to persuade me to accept this?

Useful questions to ask when *evaluating* a research paper are:

- How plausible is the reasoning and explanation that is provided?

- How reliable is the evidence on which this reasoning is based?

Record-keeping

When pupils come to do their own research, and particularly when they come to disseminate that research, they may wish to refer to the work others have done in the same field so it is worth encouraging them to adopt good record-keeping habits early on. They will find it frustrating to have to track down a year of publication, or an author's initial, long after they have sent the book back to the library or lost the electronic trail that led them to that particular source. If pupils use a direct quote from a source they *must* have the number of the page on which the quotation appears.

Keeping notes does not have to be a mammoth task. Pupils are not expected to write an essay about every research paper, chapter or book they read. Some researchers use an index card system, kept either manually or electronically, where each card holds information about author, year, title and place of publication, a couple of summary sentences and then specific page references relating to any key points or quotations that have emerged (see Box 2.2). Pupils could make their own index cards or use those provided in Photocopiable Resource 2.

BOX 2.2 INFORMATION TO PUT ON AN INDEX CARD ENTRY

Author(s) surname(s) plus initial(s)...

Year of publication ....

Title..

Publisher ....

Brief summary ....

Key point 1 (page ref)..

Key point 2, etc. (page ref)...

Good quotation(s) I might use (page ref)...

Core Activity

The core activity is essentially a guided orientation around a sample research paper. You may have lots of ideas of papers which would be suitable for the age and ability of pupils you are working with –good sources of material can be found in journals such as *Childhood* and *Children & Society*.

A recommended text for this core activity is:

Elsey, S. (2004) Children's experience of public space, *Children & Society*, 18(2): 155–164.

This is a research study about the experiences of 10–14-year-olds use of space and the extent to which their views are represented in policy decisions.

Intermediate level

Discuss the following questions:

- Is the title a good summary of the paper? If not, can you suggest a better one?
- Does the abstract tell you a little about the introduction, methodology, findings and conclusions?
- Does the introduction tell you what the study is about and why it is being undertaken? Does it review other people's research in the field?
- Is there sufficient explanation in the methodology for a replication? Is the method appropriate for the research question? Can you find anything unsound, unethical or absent from the description of the method?
- Are the results clear and presented in a way that is easy to follow and understand?
- Does the discussion section relate the findings of the study to the literature reported in the introduction? Are there ways in which it could be improved?

Choose one of the references cited in the body of the research article and check if it is referenced correctly at the end of the paper.

Differentiating the core activity

Simpler level

Using different coloured pens mark the beginning and end of each of the following:

- the title
- the abstract
- the introduction
- the method
- the findings
- the discussion
- the references.

Advanced level

In addition to the intermediate activity, write a précis of each of the sections identified above.

Information-searching Skills

Information-searching skills are very important in research. There is an excellent electronic resource called SAFARI designed by library staff at the Open University which is freely available to everyone and would be suitable for able pupils. You do not have to be affiliated to the university in order to use this resource. It is an interactive, online tutorial which takes you on a journey through the research information supply chain and helps you develop critical evaluation skills. SAFARI is divided into seven topics, each topic is divided into sections and then subdivided into pages. Some topics can be studied discretely but if pupils wanted to work through the whole programme it would take about 20 hours and this would need to be spread over one or two terms. The resource can be used individually or in pairs and is undertaken at pupils' own pace. The SAFARI programme can be accessed at www.open.ac.uk/library/SAFARI.

Expert Researcher Card Games

Make new cards for the six key research terms given in Box 2.1 and six new cards containing the glossary definitions. Pupils now have ten pairs of expert researcher cards.

Game 2: True or false?

This game can be played in pairs or in groups with a teacher or facilitator. Each player is given two cards. On the first is written 'true' and on the second is written 'false'. The teacher or game facilitator holds the collated glossary sheet with all the key words and their correct definitions (see Photocopiable Resource 12). The teacher or facilitator announces one of the key words and then reads out a definition (the teacher can choose whether this is a true or a false definition). Players have to decide whether they think the definition is true or false and hold up the appropriate card. Players get a point for every correct answer. Teachers can easily adjust the level of difficulty of this game according to the group.

Optional Extension Activity

Pupils can gain more experience by reading and discussing other research papers. A suggestion for a second paper is:

Coates, E. (2002) 'I forgot the sky!': children's stories contained within their drawings, *International Journal of Early Years*, 10(1): 21-35 .

This is a short paper which discusses the talk children engage in when drawing pictures.

Follow-up Work

A suitable follow-up task would be for pupils to read another short research paper in order to practise some of their newly acquired skills. A research study undertaken by children of a similar age would be very appropriate. Three are featured in Chapter 13 or there are several to choose from on the website of the Children's Research Centre at http://childrens-research-centre.open.ac.uk.

Key Reflection from Session 2

Helpful questions to ask when *analysing* a research paper are:

What is the author trying to get me to accept?

What evidence is the author providing to persuade me to accept this?

Helpful questions to ask when *evaluating* a research paper are:

How plausible is the reasoning and explanation that is provided?

How reliable is the evidence on which this reasoning is based?

Suggested Further Reading

Konstant, T. (2000) *Speed Reading*, London: Hodder & Stoughton.

Lewis, V., Kellett, M., Robinson, C., Fraser, S. and Ding, S. (eds) (2004) *The Reality of Research with Children and Young People*, London: Sage in association with OUP.

This book is a collection of research papers on child and youth topics illustrating the process of carrying out research. Each research study is accompanied by a commentary from the author.

CHAPTER 3

Research Ethics

Learning aims	Knowledge content	Skills	Interactive elements	Pupil follow-up work	Curriculum links
Understand the primary importance of ethics in research	Informed consent	Thinking skills	Role play	Watching video or other documentary material to stimulate reflection and discussion around ethical issues	PSHE
	Human rights	Appreciating perspectives other than one's own	Group discussion		Citizenship
Appreciate a given situation from another person's perspective	Confidentiality		Expert Researcher card games		RS
	Anonymity	Making balanced judgements			Literacy
Develop greater ethical awareness		Exploring moral and social values			Drama

TEACHING CONTENT FOR SESSION 3

Timing: 90 minutes + 45 minutes follow-up work.

Introduction

A great deal of thought and attention has to be given to the ethics of all research studies and this should not be any less rigorous just because it is children who are carrying out the research. Ethical considerations are not a 'bolt-on' option; they are an integral core of each stage from initial design through to dissemination. Sometimes, the topic of the research itself can give rise to ethical sensitivity. If, for example, the research concerns bullying, then the very act of exploring this with individuals could cause distress, anxiety or increase an individual's vulnerability to a bullying situation. On the other hand, it is important that issues like bullying are explored so that we can increase our knowledge and understanding, and hopefully improve prevention rates. In simple terms, researchers have to weigh up the possible benefits of their study against what is known as its 'costs' (Frankfort-Nachmias and Nachmias, 1992). By 'costs' we mean the personal costs, emotional, financial, physical, etc., to those involved (including the researcher). Examples of such 'costs' might be,

- *emotional* –e.g. anxiety, embarrassment, depression, loss of self-esteem
- *financial* –e.g. cost of the individual's time, loss of earnings, travel costs
- *physical* –e.g. pain or other physical effects (e.g. in medical research).

Weighing up the cost-benefits ratio is one of the ethical aspects to consider at the design stage of a research study. There are many others. Some of the guiding principles which Alderson and Morrow (2004) invite us to focus on include:

- respect and justice –e.g. respecting participants' sensitivities and dignities
- rights –e.g. participants' rights to be protected from harm, to be fully informed and to be listened to
- best outcomes –to actively promote best outcomes for participants.

Ethics operate at macro and micro levels throughout and beyond the life of a research study. The macro level is generally a process of approval by an ethics committee, or similar body, where research proposals are scrutinised for anything unethical and committees sometimes insist on changes being made to the design of the study before approval can be granted. Ethics committees provide a formal set of guidelines. These can prove useful ethical checklists for new researchers. Guidelines issued by the British Educational Research Association are available on their website at www.bera.co.uk.

At a micro level, researchers constantly make individual, fine judgements about ethical sensitivities relating to participants, e.g. whether a particular interview question might cause them distress.

Informed Consent

All research requires the consent of those participating. Before individuals can give their consent they need some understanding of what is involved and exactly what they are consenting to. This is what we call *informed consent*. Simply saying 'I'm doing some research on teenage magazine culture' and asking individuals to sign consent forms is *not* sufficient and is ethically questionable. Participants should be told the aims and objectives of the research, how the data collected from them will be used (especially with regard to confidentiality and anonymity) and how the findings will be disseminated. All of this information should be transparent, with no hidden agendas. In the example of the teenage magazine culture a researcher might declare that her objective is to explore the relationship between celebrity mania and teenage girls' self-image; that she intends to use the interview data she collects to analyse whether celebrity mania has a predominantly positive or negative effect on body image and to disseminate her findings to health departments.

However, the issue of informed consent with regard to participating children is complex because of their 'minority status' and therefore informed consent is required from those who have legal care and control – a parent, guardian or local authority. Sometimes there can be a conflict of interest. Children may wish to participate in a study but parents refuse consent. In most cases, parental wishes take precedence but there are some exceptions, especially where older children are concerned. Legally, a child is a minor until the age of 18, but some rights are obtained at 16. There have been some famous legal precedents set where young people have won the right to overturn parents' wishes. One such example has become known as the 'Gillick ruling'. In the leading case, *Gillick* v. *W. Norfolk and Wisbech* (1985) the House of Lords upheld the view that a child who has sufficient understanding can consent to medical treatment, and that a parent of such a child has no right to override the child's consent.

The debates rage on about the age at which children are deemed responsible enough to give their informed consent and about when this should become a requirement in addition to any consent given by their parents, irrespective of their age. Although 5-year-olds may not be able to sign a consent form, this does not remove an obligation to explain, as far as possible and in language the child can understand, what the research study is about. From an ethical point of view, as opposed to a purely legal point of view, it is desirable for all children to be approached about giving their consent. Any risks or problems associated with the study should be explained, along with a brief summary of the methods and a time plan. It is becoming increasingly popular to produce child-friendly leaflets setting out information about the research study.

Informed consent also relates to *ongoing* consent in that participants should understand that they can withdraw their consent at any time and for any reason. Informed consent which is ethically obtained does not involve any element of coercion on the part of the researcher. This is particularly relevant in contexts where participants are relatively powerless –e.g. children in schools or elderly patients in residential homes. There are many examples of unethical coercive practice, e.g. suggesting to prisoners that participation might increase their chances of parole, or that non-participation might adversely affect a child's chances of being picked for the school football team or that participation might be viewed favourably by those who influence career promotion.

Deception

Can deception ever be justified in research? Some writers argue that the answer is an unequivocal no. Others argue that there are occasions when ends justify the means and where the ultimate 'benefits' outweigh any deception 'costs'. But deception is never a good basis on which to build an exploration of truth and knowledge and it is difficult to think of occasions when this kind of covert activity should ever be undertaken in the name of research. Certainly, it is not something we would want to be encouraging child researchers to engage in. An example of deception used in research is covert observation via hidden cameras or two-way mirrors. Other examples include situations where researchers deceive participants about the true purpose of their research, e.g. if a researcher asks to collect data via classroom observation pretending that the research is about pupils' attention spans when in fact the researcher is collecting data about teachers' questioning styles.

Confidentiality and Anonymity

There is an ethical duty to protect participants from public scrutiny. Wherever possible researchers assure participants that the data they collect will be treated confidentially and anonymity preserved. Names are changed when the study is reported. Special care is taken with video data because this is more difficult to make anonymous. Because of this, video and photographic data are sometimes destroyed at the end of a research study to ensure anonymity. Box 3.1 gives some examples of questionable practices in social research.

Core Activity

The core activity for Session 3 is a role-play activity designed to help pupils engage with some of the conflicts and tensions that result from many ethical dilemmas. This works best with small groups of about six pupils but 'roles' can be added to accommodate larger numbers. Pupils need to familiarise themselves with the ethical dilemma depicted in the scenario in Box 3.2 (also see Photocopiable Resource 3).

BOX 3.1 EXAMPLES OF QUESTIONABLE PRACTICES IN SOCIAL RESEARCH

1 Involving people without their knowledge or consent.
2 Coercing them to participate.
3 Withholding information about the true nature of the research.
4 Otherwise deceiving the participant.
5 Inducing participants to commit acts diminishing their self-esteem.
6 Violating rights of self-determination (e.g. in studies seeking to promote individual change).
7 Exposing participants to physical or mental stress.
8 Invading privacy.
9 Withholding benefits from some participants (e.g. in comparison groups).
10 Not treating participants fairly, or with consideration, or with respect.

(Robson, 2002: 69)

BOX 3.2 AN ETHICAL DILEMMA

An 11-year-old boy, Joséf, is dying from a very rare form of cancer. There is no known cure and he only has a few months left to live. Researchers are in the process of developing a new drug which they think may be able to cure this cancer in the future if it could be caught at an early enough stage. The drug is not perfected yet and even if it were, Joséf's cancer is already far too advanced for it to be able to cure him. However, doctors could learn a lot more about the drug and its potential if they could test it out on Joséf. Although this would not help Joséf it could benefit many more children in the future. There is a possibility that there might be some side effects from the drug but the doctors cannot be sure as it has not been tested on humans before. Joséf's parents are against this and are refusing to give their consent. They want Joséf to have the best possible quality of life and to be left in peace for the few months he has left. But Joséf would like to help the doctors and says he wants to do some good with his life before he dies. Who should have the final say on consent? Should Joséf, aged 11, be allowed to overrule his parents or should his parents wishes prevail? Who else might influence the decision-making process?

A role play can be enacted with the following parts and pupils can repeat the activity taking turns to play different roles.

Josef   Wants to have the drug and insists it's his body and his life.

Mother Wants Josef to be left in peace so that the family can make the most of the little time they have left together.

Father   Angry that the doctors should have approached them with this proposal, says this is emotional blackmail and that Josef is being exploited.

Sister   Supports Josef.

Doctor Arguing for the possible benefits for other children.

Nurse   Undecided.

Additional roles for larger numbers: younger sibling, grandparent(s), second nurse.

Expert Researcher Card Games

There are no additional key research terms from this session to make cards for but a variation on the game can still be introduced using the ten pairs of cards you already have.

Game 3: Memory pairs

Shuffle the cards and place them face down on the table. In pairs, players take turns to uncover two cards trying to find a match for a key research term with its correct definition. If a player is successful, she or he gets to keep the matched pair, if not the cards are replaced face down in exactly the same position on the table.

Optional Extension Activity

As an optional extension activity pupils may wish to read the ethics chapter by Priscilla Alderson featured in the suggested further reading at the end of Chapter 2.

Follow-up Work

Follow-up work can be based around pupil discussion groups or written reflections. Suitable stimulus material can be found from archive sources around ethical issues. For example, there are many television documentaries which cover controversial situations where children are involved in research. Depending on the ages of pupils these might be drawn from documentaries such as the BBC's *Child of Our Time* (10–12-year-olds), *Panorama* (12–14-year-olds), or from regional news report specials or library archive material. Archive footage of research experiments can be found in libraries and on the Internet, e.g. for older pupils transcript extracts from the controversial Stephen Ceci research about the reliability of child witness statements can be accessed by keying in 'Stephen Ceci' into a reliable Internet search engine.

Key Reflection from Session 3

Ethical considerations are of paramount importance in any research activity. They should not be viewed as a 'bolt-on' option but as an integral core of each stage of the research from initial design through to dissemination.

Suggested Further Reading

Alderson, P. and Morrow, V. (2004) *Ethics, Social Research and Consulting with Children and Young People*, Barkingside: Barnado's.

Morrow, V. and Richards, M. (1996). The ethics of social research with children: an overview, *Children & Society*, 10(2): 90–105.

Christensen, P. and Prout, A. (2002) Working with ethical symmetry in social research with children, *Childhood*, 9(4): 477–497.

CHAPTER 4

Framing a Research Question

Learning aims	Knowledge content	Skills	Interactive elements	Pupil follow-up work	Curriculum links
Begin to understand what a research question is and how it differs from a hypothesis Begin to understand how a research question informs the design and data collection methods of a research study	The pivotal place of a research question in research process	Question framing Sorting the essential from the peripheral and/or irrelevant Funnelling techniques	Group discussion Expert Researcher card games	Children's research featured on websites	Science Literacy

TEACHING CONTENT FOR SESSION 4

Timing: 60 minutes + 20 minutes follow-up work.

Introduction

Before pupils can begin to think about how they will go about collecting data for their research study they need to frame a research question and, if appropriate, formulate a hypothesis(es). If the research question is not carefully worked out in advance then the wrong kinds of data may be collected. Of course, some types of ethnographic research have very loose frameworks because of their open and exploratory nature, and in some instances research questions do not emerge until much later in the process. However, most small-scale research that school pupils will engage in is likely to need a tightly worded research question at the outset. In part, this is to help pupils design a study that they will be able to complete in a term. Ownership of the study is a significant motivating factor and pupils are more likely to complete their study and stick at it if the parameters are small scale and realistic. Posing a research question sets the framework for the whole project, giving it direction and coherence. Allow plenty of discussion time when pupils can play around with ideas and discover what is at the heart of what they want to find out. This is what is called a 'funnelling-down' process and starts with a pupil's general interest in a particular topic and gradually reduces down by stages to the core of a question. Throughout this process it is helpful to keep focusing on

What am I trying to find out?

Some pupils already have fixed ideas of the area they want to research and the teacher's role is to refine these ideas into a manageable project with a focused research question. Other pupils are much vaguer and need encouragement to crystallise their ideas. A 'think sheet' can be a useful tool in these circumstances and you will find a blank template for a 'think sheet' if you turn to Photocopiable Resource 4 at the end of this book. Box 4.1 contains an example of a completed 'think sheet' by a 12-year-old boy.

The Funnelling Process

Frequently, the posing of a question will lead to the formulation of a hypothesis(es) to test out the question. This leads the researcher to determine what data are appropriate to collect in order to test out the hypothesis. For example, a pupil Marcia is interested in the issue of homework. From this general topic she needs to decide what area within that topic is of particular interest. Group sounding boards and teacher support can help Marcia in the funnelling process with rhetorical-style questioning. For instance, is the primary area of interest around:

- the amount of homework pupils have to do?
- the relevance of the homework?
- the nature of the homework (how boring/interesting it is)?
- how long pupils spend on homework?
- pupils' views about homework?

Marcia decides she is mainly interested in pupils' views about homework. This is the first stage of the funnelling process achieved. Further stages of Marcia's funnelling process might look like this:

→ *Am I interested in a particular age?*

Yes and no – I'm sort of interested in whether attitudes change as pupils get older.

→ *So am I interested in comparing two ages?*

Yes, I think so.

→ *Which particular ages?*

Probably Year 4 and Year 6. There might be some differences because Year 6 pupils will soon be moving up to secondary school and they have important tests to do.

→ *Am I also interested in whether there are any gender differences in attitudes?*

Yes, I'd be really interested to see if girls and boys view homework differently and whether girls seem to spend longer on their homework than boys.

→ *What about how pupils feel about their parents' attitude to their homework?*

Yes, I'd be interested to see if pupils want parents to take an interest in their homework and want them to help or whether they feel resentful at being 'supervised'.

From this initial exploration Marcia comes up with a research question:

Are attitudes to homework different in Year 4 and Year 6 pupils?

She formulates these hypotheses from this question:

- Year 6s mind less about having to do homework.
- Most children like their parents to be involved in their homework.
- Most girls spend longer on their homework than boys.

She decides the title for her project will be:

Investigating the views of Year 4 and Year 6 pupils to homework.

At this point Marcia then has to think about how she will go about collecting data to answer her research question. There are many different methods she could consider. When developing children as researchers it is important to train them in a range of methods so that they can make an informed choice

BOX 4.1 EXAMPLE OF A COMPLETED 'THINK SHEET'

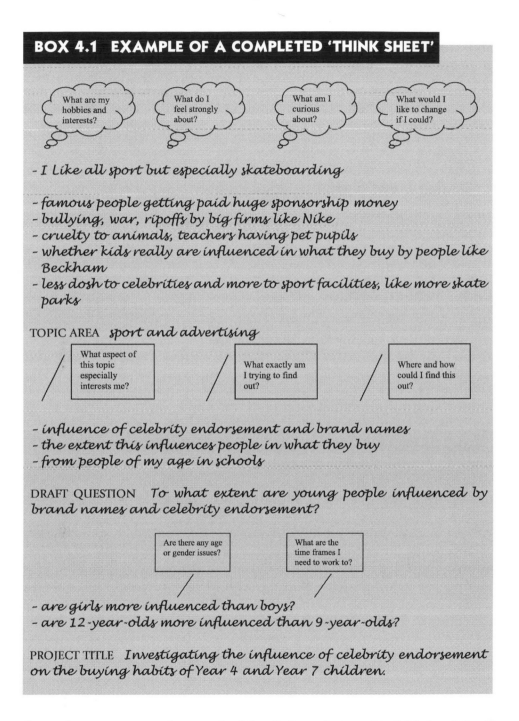

What are my hobbies and interests?

What do I feel strongly about?

What am I curious about?

What would I like to change if I could?

- I like all sport but especially skateboarding

- famous people getting paid huge sponsorship money
- bullying, war, ripoffs by big firms like Nike
- cruelty to animals, teachers having pet pupils
- whether kids really are influenced in what they buy by people like Beckham
- less dosh to celebrities and more to sport facilities, like more skate parks

TOPIC AREA sport and advertising

What aspect of this topic especially interests me?

What exactly am I trying to find out?

Where and how could I find this out?

- influence of celebrity endorsement and brand names
- the extent this influences people in what they buy
- from people of my age in schools

DRAFT QUESTION To what extent are young people influenced by brand names and celebrity endorsement?

Are there any age or gender issues?

What are the time frames I need to work to?

- are girls more influenced than boys?
- are 12-year-olds more influenced than 9-year-olds?

PROJECT TITLE Investigating the influence of celebrity endorsement on the buying habits of Year 4 and Year 7 children.

about the most appropriate method for their study. Part II of this book is all about data collection techniques.

Core Activity

Use either your own prompt sheet or the 'think sheet' from Photocopiable Resource 4 to encourage pupils to decide on a focus for their research, and if possible a draft research question. Pupils can form their own support groups for this activity.

Expert Researcher Card Games

There are no new Expert Researcher cards to prepare from this chapter but pupils can try out a new game with the existing cards.

Game 4: Blind auction

This game works best with two players. In addition to the current Expert Researcher cards you will need one set of number cards with values 0-7 for each player. The idea of the game is to pair up as many cards in your hand with its matching key term or glossary definition. The winner is the player with the greatest number of matched cards when the auction is finished.

Shuffle the cards and deal out seven cards to each player. Put the remaining cards in the centre of the table and turn the top card face up. This card then becomes the object of a blind auction between the two players. They decide (secretly) how much they will bid for the card and accordingly place one of their number cards (from 0-7) face down in front of them. Simultaneously the two players turn over their number cards and the higher value wins the auctioned card. A player's number card can only be used once and must be discarded after the blind bidding round is completed. For example, if a player uses a number '4' card, this must be discarded irrespective of whether he or she won the auctioned card. Therefore players have to think carefully about how much they want to 'bid' for a particular card. If they have the matching card in their hand it would make sense to bid on the high side. If they do not have the matching card, then its match is either in the opponent's hand or still in the pile in the centre of the table and they need to either play safe with a low bid (e.g. the 0 or 1 card could be used) and gamble on the matched card turning up in the centre pack and being able to win it when it is auctioned. If two players turn over the same number card, they must return their number cards to their packs and try again. This process can be repeated until there is a clear auction winner.

Optional Extension Activity

Pupils can be directed to one of the author commentaries in the edited collection of research papers featured as suggested further reading at the end of Chapter 2 (Lewis et al., 2004). These author commentaries illuminate some of the 'behind-the-scenes' thinking processes that precede a research study, including some of the funnelling processes covered in the teaching content of this chapter.

Follow-up Work

Pupils will benefit from as many opportunities to engage with other people's research as possible. Examples of projects with participating children and young people can be found on the websites of organisations such as Save The Children, Carnegie-Youth Trust and the Children's Society. There are also some suggestions at the end of this chapter.

Key Reflection from Session 4

Posing a research question(s) sets the framework for the whole project, gives it direction and coherence and determines the method(s) of data collection.

Suggested Further Reading

Some examples of research involving children and young people are:

Howarth, R. (1997) *If We Don't Play Now, When Can We?* London: Hopscotch Asian Women's Centre.

Jones, A., Jeyasingham, D. and Rajasooriya, S. (2002) *Invisible Families: The Strengths and Needs of Black Families in Which Young People Have Caring Responsibilities*, Bristol: Policy Press and Joseph Rowntree Foundation.

P ART II

Data Collection

Observation Techniques

Learning aims	Knowledge content	Skills	Interactive elements	Pupil follow-up work	Curriculum links
To develop observation skills	Systematic observation Naturalistic observation Observation in real and suspended time	Observe, describe and accurately record data Devise coding categories	Observation activities Video filming Coding activities Expert Researcher card games	Observation practice Video filming practice	Science PSHE Humanities IT

TEACHING CONTENT FOR SESSION 5

Timing: 90 minutes + 30 minutes follow-up work.

Naturalistic Observation

Observation can be undertaken in several ways and with differing levels of researcher involvement. Naturalistic observation occurs where the observer does nothing to manipulate or stimulate the behaviour of the individuals being observed, aiming for as natural and typical a situation as possible. Supposing you were interested in researching ways in which young children interact with an older sibling. Naturalistic observation would involve observing the two siblings in an environment that was typical and where they would 'naturally' have opportunities to interact together –e.g. at a mealtime in their home environment. Naturalistic observation can be undertaken either from the outside looking in –like being a 'fly on the wall' –or from the inside looking around.

The former, 'outside looking in' style of observation, aims to be objective and avoid becoming part of the 'action being observed' because this changes the dynamics of that action and might interfere with, or alter, the behaviour of those being observed. It has to be accepted that there can never be absolute objectivity for two reasons. First, unless deception is involved – which we already established in Chapter 3 was not a desirable situation – there is bound to be a small degree of 'interference' in any given situation simply by the very presence of an observer (or camera), however unobtrusive this is intended to be. Secondly, observers are continuously making subjective judgements about what they are seeing, so even at this primary stage of observation there is some initial filtering of the data going on. With human beings, a low level of filtering is inevitable and the important thing is to be aware of it, acknowledge it and record the circumstances in which the data are being collected, thus rendering the method transparent and open to scrutiny by others. If you are not using a video recorder, always make notes of your observations at the time. Retrospective observation notes are subject to challenges of 'hindsight adjustments' and can invalidate your research.

Participant Observation

The 'inside looking around' style of observation is generally called participant observation because the researchers are actually a part of the action they are observing. In the example given above – investigating the social interaction between younger and older siblings –the researcher might be a sibling in the family or perhaps a parent and, therefore, her or his presence is bound to have an impact on the nature of the action. There is a dual role at work here, e.g. observing and parenting, and one cannot be divorced from the other, therefore the participatory aspect must be acknowledged from the outset. The process of being aware of our position as researcher and how this affects the nature of what we are studying is called being *reflexive*.

An example of non-participant, naturalistic observation might be a researcher, who has no prior involvement with a particular school class, using observation as a method to explore gender differences in the way children in that class use computers. Here, the data are collected from typical class lessons without setting up any special situations, groupings or predetermined tasks. The same research question, if investigated by the class teacher, would become participatory observation. Other examples of participant observation might be a researcher using observation to investigate the effectiveness of a school council, while they are members of that council or a study using observation to explore the nature of class friendship groups by someone who is a member of that class.

Systematic Observation

Systematic observation is a term used to describe a particularly rigorous style of observation which may or may not involve the manipulation or stimulation of behaviour. It is a meticulous method in which the minutiae of behaviour are targeted for observation and requires a degree of pre-planning because researchers need to know what particular aspects of behaviour they are going to be looking at, rather than just observing generally. In quantitative research there has to be a process of translating observations into numerical data. This is usually done by a coding procedure. Certain aspects of behaviour are categorised or coded so that they can be measured. Depending on the nature of the research this might be done *before* the observation or *after* the observation.

Supposing pupils want to investigate teacher questioning styles in the classroom and are particularly interested in teachers' use of open and closed questions. They would need to observe some lessons being taught and it would be sensible to set up two codes *before* the observation, one for open questions and one for closed questions. At the simplest level they could record a tally of the number of open and closed questions a teacher uses in any given lesson, as shown in Table 5.1.

Table 5.1   Incidence of open and closed teacher questions

Teacher	Subject	Lesson length	Open questions	Closed questions
Mr Stiles	History	40 minutes	12	8
Ms Fox	Maths	40 minutes	5	13
Mrs Beaver	Religious Studies	40 minutes	16	7
Mr Croll	Physics (practical)	80 minutes	16	16
Dr Porter	English	40 minutes	10	6

There are likely to be many additional aspects of teacher questioning styles they may be interested in. For example, they might want to observe how encouraging or discouraging a teacher's body language is when posing a question. This would be more easily coded *after* the observation because they would not necessarily know what they were looking for initially. Post-observation coding can be done in two ways: either from analysing their notes and then sorting these into 'themes' or categories, or, if the observations were video-recorded, coding from further viewings of the data. For example, if, during a post-viewing of a video-recorded lesson, they noticed that when asking a closed question the teacher frequently waved her pen towards the class and sometimes also adopted a 'fixed stare', whereas, when asking an open question, she gestured with an open hand and tended to raise her eyebrows slightly. This could be explored further by measuring the number of instances when this occurs and in what circumstances (see Table 5.2).

Table 5.2 Incidence tally of teacher questioning styles

Teacher	Behaviour	Closed questions	Open questions	Other	Total
Ms Fox	Points	9	0	5	12
	Waves pen	6	2	7	15
	Hands on hip	5	0	4	9
	Raises eyebrows	0	4	2	6
	Open hand gesture	0	3	5	8
	Folds arms	7	0	3	10

Systematic observation is not solely concerned with the number of instances of something happening. It is also important to think about the duration of these behaviours and the circumstances in which they happen. Supposing pupils wanted to code 'shouting' behaviour during a wet morning break time and supposing their observations reveal five instances of shouting by child *a* and two instances of shouting by child *b*. By simply counting the number of incidences they might conclude that child *a* shouted more than child *b*. However, if they were to measure the duration of each shouting incident they might come to a different conclusion. An example is given in Table 5.3 where start times and finish times of the shouting are recorded. This is sometimes referred to as *on-set* and *off-set* timing. The on-set being the start of the behaviour and the off-set being the end of the behaviour.

Table 5.3 Incidence and duration of 'shouting' for child *a* and child *b*

Child *a*	On-set time		Off-set time		Duration	Child *b*	On-set time		Off-set time		Duration
	mins	secs	mins	secs	secs		mins	secs	mins	secs	secs
	1	27	1	36	9		3	44	4	29	45
	5	33	5	46	13		8	13	8	56	43
	7	20	7	25	5						
	11	17	11	28	11						
	12	10	12	14	4						
Total					42 secs						88 secs

It is also important to know in what circumstances the shouting behaviour occurred. For example, child *a*'s shouting might have occurred in response to another child shouting at him, or following a physical attack on him, or because there was so much noise it was difficult to make himself heard, or perhaps he was trying to prevent someone else from being hurt. The researcher would then have to decide whether to pre-code for these differences or to make notes alongside the measurements. Examples of situations where a researcher might use this kind of approach could be investigating aggressive behaviour in the playground or exploring disaffected behaviour in lessons.

Time to Recap

Thus there are different degrees of structure which can be applied to observation techniques. Quantitative methods tend to be highly structured and, as detailed above, have categories of what to look for in advance so that these can be measured. Sometimes this can involve the use of standardised coding categories which have been devised by other people and used in other situations. A structured approach commonly breaks down behaviour into smaller parts and observes the minutiae of this. For example, observation of facial activity may be broken down into smaller behavioural segments such as eye contact, smiling, etc. Qualitative methods tend to be less structured and rarely use predetermined categories but describe events in a more open-ended way as they naturally occur. An unstructured approach looks at the larger picture.

BOX 5.1 KEY RESEARCH TERMS FOR SESSION 5

naturalistic observation: the observer does nothing to manipulate or stimulate the behaviour of the individuals being observed, aiming for as natural and typical a situation as possible.

participant observation: observation undertaken by a researcher who is also part of the action being observed, usually, but not always, associated with a qualitative approach.

reflexive: a process of reflecting on the researcher's own position in relation to the action being investigated and the impact this might have on the collection of data and the analysis of findings.

systematic observation: a meticulous method in which the minutiae of behaviour is targeted for observation and measured via a coding system.

Observation in Real Time and Suspended Time

Another important distinction to be made is between the two conditions of observation in *real time* and observation in *suspended time*. Observation in real time relates to observations which are made in the moment of them happening and recorded at the time of them happening. Observation in suspended time relates to data which are collected, usually by video recording, and then observed at a later time – hence the term 'suspended time' – often being viewed several times over. There are advantages and disadvantages in both methods and pupils should select the one which is most appropriate for their study, in other words the one which will enable them to collect the right kind of information to best answer their research question(s). Let us look at a specific example.

An Example of Observation in Real Time

Supposing, Sasha, as an elected pupil member of a school council, is party to a discussion about improving pupil behaviour in the classroom. The discussion focuses on what new rules and sanctions could be introduced to improve behaviour. Sasha makes the point that new rules are not necessarily the answer because he thinks that a lot of the bad behaviour in his classroom is brought about through pupil boredom. The Council are interested in Sasha's opinion and want him to do a small piece of research on this and report back to the Council. As part of his investigation Sasha decides to undertake some classroom observation.

He decides to do this in real time as it will be less disruptive. He obtains all the necessary consents from pupils and staff to do this. However, he realises it will be very difficult to observe the behaviour of all 33 pupils at the same time so he decides to focus on just one pupil, Manzoor, initially.

Next, Sasha has to decide whether he is going to observe in a structured or an unstructured way. With unstructured observation he would watch Manzoor throughout the lesson and describe exactly what he sees, e.g. whether Manzoor is looking at the teacher and listening to the teacher, whether he is messing about or chatting to his mates, engaging in any bad behaviour or breaking any school rules. Does Manzoor appear bored or interested in the content of the lesson? If he is asked a question how does he answer –rudely, politely, aggressively, timidly, rebelliously? When asked to do a task, does Manzoor get on with it or not? Does he seem to be enjoying the task or bored by it? Does the task appear to be too difficult for him or too easy?

When engaging in real time observation, many researchers use dictation machines to enable them to record their data without taking their eyes away from the focus of their observation. This involves transcribing the data at a later time. In Sasha's situation, however, this would prove disruptive to the lesson so he records his observations by handwritten notes.

However, with structured observation, Sasha would decide in advance what specific aspects of behaviour he is going to observe and then record every instance of this. He might choose categories such as *bored, interested* and *disruptive.* To measure these behaviours he would need to count the number of instances and time the duration of each one. Some data is presented in Table 5.4 to illustrate this for a lesson which started at 11.00 a.m. and ended at 11.40 a.m.

Table 5.4 Structured observation of Manzoor

Start time	Bored Finish time	Total	Interested Start time	Finish time	Total	Disruptive/bad behaviour Start Time	Finish time	Total
11.00	11.06	6 mins						
						11.06	11.08	2 mins
			11.08	11.13	5 mins			
11.13	11.18	5 mins						
						11.19	11.23	4 mins
			11.23	11.28	5 mins			
						11.28	11.29	1 min
11.29	11.35	6 mins						
						11.36	11.40	4 mins
		19 min			10 min			11 min

This kind of structured observation is quite difficult to do in real time and is more commonly done in suspended time after the observations have been video-recorded. From the small example given in Table 5.4 you can see how illuminating systematic observation can be, not just in terms of incidence and duration but also *sequence*. If you look carefully at the data in Table 5.4, you will notice that three out of the four instances of disruptive/bad behaviour immediately followed bored behaviour.

Video can provide a very detailed record of events as they happen. So video can be a very valuable tool for observational research. This approach is described as 'observation in suspended time', because the events can be observed and re-observed many times. The aim of *naturalistic observation* is to record events as they unfold, as if you were a 'fly on the wall'. For example, if pupils wanted to carry out research into children starting school, they might want to observe a child's first experiences of arriving into their new classroom. Later, they could make a detailed qualitative analysis of what happened, who spoke to the child, how the child reacted, and so on.

Using Video to Collect Observation Data in Suspended Time

Video can be a useful tool for collecting both quantitative and qualitative data. For example, if pupils were carrying out research into mixed gender football, they could make a recording of part of a game. Then, at a later time, they could count precisely how many passes were made by boys to boys, boys to girls, girls to girls or girls to boys. This is a quantitative approach. Video can also be used qualitatively, e.g. if pupils want to observe facial expressions or peer behaviour in the playground. Sometimes, video is also used to record interviews, but mostly an audio recording or detailed notes are much more practical. However, a video recording of the interview is useful when facial expressions and bodily gestures are important to the research question. If pupils are using MiniDV, these recordings can be imported into a computer. Short sequences identified as particularly important can then be played back 'frame by frame' and even slowed down if more intricate analysis is required.

Tips for Collecting Observation Data by Video Camera

Useful video recordings are easier to make in situations where people and events are not moving too fast, where pupils can keep track of what is happening and anticipate what is about to happen. For example, it is quite difficult to record children moving around in a large playground, unless pupils can make the recording from a first floor window where they can 'capture' the whole playground in one shot. There is another reason for being cautious about video filming in large spaces where there are large numbers of people. This is that a major problem for all video-based research is ensuring researchers can hear what is being said. The microphone picks up everything indiscriminately and it cannot filter out sounds which researchers are not interested in, such as traffic noise. So, pupils may get beautifully framed pictures but with a soundtrack of dogs barking, traffic noise and a hubbub of talk, including anything they say themselves while they are recording. Although the zoom lens can bring the picture up close, there is no equivalent zoom on the microphone. Sound is usually better when a smaller number of people are involved, and they are not all talking at once.

- Wherever possible use the tripod, or rest the camera on a firm surface.

- Record sequences of at least 30 seconds.

- Once you have planned a shot, hold the camera steady, or move it very slowly when recording;

- Use the zoom to establish the shot, but do not keep zooming in and out during recording.

Sometimes, video makes observation more difficult, not easier. Modern cameras are quite small, but they are still cameras. People often become very self-conscious when they think they are being filmed, and they may 'act-up' for the camera. A researcher is unlikely to be ignored as a 'fly on the wall' if she or he has a video camera in her or his hand. Sometimes, people can get used to the camera after a while, so pupils may want to do a few practice recordings before they begin serious observation.

Making the recording is only the beginning. Researchers then have to analyse and make sense of the recording. This can be very time-consuming. The golden rule is to record a small number of short, well-planned observations. Do not just switch the camera on and leave it running until the battery or tape runs out. For example, take the mixed gender football example. Researchers might consider sampling the match (e.g. recording for one minute out of each five minutes of play) rather than the whole game, or choosing to video a five-minute block in the middle of the game.

Sometimes using a digital still camera can provide a more useful source of data than video. For example, if researchers are interested in children's play in the school playground, (e.g. whom they play with, which games they play, etc.) they could take a sequence of ten shots of a 'target pupil' over ten minutes during break time. This is much easier to analyse than a long video sequence.

Ethical Issues When Using Video Recording

Ethical issues are very important if pupils plan to use video in research. Informed consent is especially important because anonymity is more difficult to achieve for video work. It is not easy to disguise the identity of people on video. They may even refer to each other by name. For this reason, confidentiality becomes especially important. Research videos should be kept in a safe place, and they should be deleted as soon as pupils have completed the analysis, unless they have specific permission to use a sequence, e.g. as part of a research presentation. Revisit Chapter 3 if pupils want to refresh their memory about the wider ethical considerations when undertaking research.

Core Activity

Intermediate level

For this activity we are going to stay with the Manzoor example referred to earlier. Photocopiable Resource 5 contains short extracts from three written accounts of unstructured observations by different child researchers. Read through each of these and discuss the relative merits of their recording styles.

Guided comment

From Extract 1 we can deduce that Jade is a novice researcher who is simply writing down in full 'narrative format' not only what she sees but also what she is thinking. Most of the written account is irrelevant to the observation of Manzoor. Almost all of the text can be discarded as irrelevant –even the name of the school because this would only be necessary if lessons in more than one school were being observed. The prose style writing slows down the recording process to the point where this observer has missed noticing several important pieces of observation data which the other two observers spotted. The shaded areas in Box 5.2 denote written entries that are irrelevant to the observation purpose.

The second extract makes use of some shorthand techniques, uses punctuation only if it is essential for clarity and starts a new line for each new observation. Furthermore, Jack has focused solely on the observation purpose and has avoided reporting behaviour that originates from himself or pupils other than Manzoor. Certain entries, such as dialogue, are noted in full because these have to be entirely accurate if they are to be used as examples to support any discussion points. The result is a good account, with very little irrelevant data. The shaded areas in Box 5.3 show where Jack could have been more economical.

The third extract is written very economically without compromising the quality and detail of the observations so that Indra can spend the maximum amount of time watching Manzoor. She has developed a personalised shorthand notation which uses single symbols, letters or figures to replace whole words e.g. she uses the symbol ☽ as pictorial shorthand for 'around'. Other techniques used include conflating common parts of words such as *'ing'* to *'g'*. Given the rapid speed with which children send text messages and the highly developed abbreviated shorthand that is evolving as a phone text language, today's generation of children should be particularly skilled at devising their own shorthand for recording observation notes. Any kind of personalised shorthand can be used as long as the researcher can understand what has been recorded and is prepared to transcribe these into fully written out notes if they are to be used as evidence in a research report.

BOX 5.2   IRRELEVANCIES IN JADE'S OBERVATION NOTES

Bretby School, Class 7G, Observation of Manzoor during Geography lesson with supply teacher, Wednesday 21st January 2004 10.20 am

... It's been drizzling with rain all day so far and it looks like it will be wet break again. I'm sitting here waiting for the supply teacher to arrive. Mrs Jackson, our Geography teacher has been off with the flu all week - or so we're told!! - so I don't know who we'll be getting today. The teacher arrives. It's a lady supply teacher, quite old. Manzoor looks up to see who's come in. Manzoor starts to listen. The teacher asks a question and Manzoor looks around to see who's putting up their hand. Manzoor digs around in his pocket and pulls out his mobile phone. He puts it under the table where the teacher can't see it and starts to text. He is listening to the teacher again now. Manzoor is reading from his text book .... Dean's just asked me if he can borrow my gel pen, I told him not to bother me when I'm doing important observing for my research...

Differentiation ideas for the core activity

Simpler level

- In each extract, cross out anything you think it was not necessary to record. Which extract has the most crossings out? Why is this?

- Discuss why you think Jade missed some of the data that was collected by Jack and Indra.

- Look for an example of something that Indra noticed that the others did not.

Advanced level

- Write down everything that Jack noticed that Jade missed.
- Write down everything that Indra noticed that Jack missed.
- Discuss the importance of these omissions in relation to the conclusions that each observer might have drawn from their data.

BOX 5.3 IRRELEVANCIES IN JACK'S OBSERVATION NOTES

Bretby School, Class 7G, Observing Manzoor (Geography lesson), Wednesday 21st Jan 04 10.20 am

Teacher arrives

Manzoor looks up, nudges Paul next to him, nods towards Teacher and whispers something

Manzoor starts to listen

Teacher asks Manzoor a question, M looks around to see who's putting up their hand

Manzoor chewing pencil

M starts doodling

M gets out mobile phone under the table & starts texting

M begins to listen again

M turns round to chat to Ali

M realises he should be reading something from his text book

M asks P what page it is

M finds page and starts to read

Reads (about 2 mins)

Looks up to see what T is doing (handing out worksheets)

T asks him what he's doing out of his seat 'just dropped me pencil Miss' (smirking)

Sits down again, laughing and looking round to see which of his mates are watching him

Reads a bit more ...

Advantages and Disadvantages of Observing in Suspended Time

As was discussed in the section 'Using video to collect observation data in suspended time', it is increasingly common for researchers to video-record their observation data. This produces a permanent record which can be returned to over and over again, and is a popular choice for systematic observation. Having a permanent record means that, if researchers choose to, they can look at just one aspect of behaviour at a time rather than having to try and observe several aspects simultaneously. Codes can be created and added to at any time during this process. And once researchers start to analyse these, other ideas often occur, and the data can be revisited in the light of these new ideas. This is not possible with real-time observation data because they cannot re-create the original situation.

It may seem that there cannot possibly be any advantages of real-time over suspended-time observation because of the enormous advantage of having a permanent record of the data. However, this should not be regarded as a foregone conclusion and pupils need to weigh up carefully what data they need to collect and why, and what effect the presence of a camera might have on the individuals being observed before deciding between real and suspended time observation.

Advantages of video-recorded observation data

- Permanent record of the data.
- No need to make lengthy written notes.
- Individual incidents can be slowed down, paused and revisited to determine the accuracy of an observation.
- Observations can be checked by independent viewers.
- Data can be revisited for different observations as new ideas emerge from initial observations and analysis.
- The video data themselves can be used as illustrations when findings are being presented to an audience (provided all the necessary consents have been obtained).

Disadvantages of video-recorded observation data

- Video camera equipment can be expensive.
- A static video camera, positioned on a tripod, can only record a certain field of vision and needs to be set up very strategically to capture precisely what researchers are hoping to observe.
- A movable camera requires someone to operate it and if that

is the researcher then she or he cannot observe anything else at the same time.

- If researchers cannot get the camera to respond quickly enough to a new incident, you may miss it –the human eye scans much more efficiently and responds more rapidly.

- Some cameras are not good at picking up sound, and all sounds are recorded indiscriminately –the human ear is much better at filtering out unimportant background noises and homing in on speech.

- Participants may be less willing to give their consent if they know a permanent video record is being made. Consent issues also become more involved to ensure that participants are fully informed about how precisely the video data will be used. Complex ethical situations can arise where parents initially give permission for their young children to be video-recorded but as those children get older they exercise their right to dissent.

- Ownership of video data can also be a legal and ethical minefield –who owns the video data, the researcher or the individuals in the video?

In practice, many researchers use both methods, making use of a static video camera, positioned on a tripod, to collect a permanent record while simultaneously taking observation notes in real time.

Expert Researcher Card Games

Make new cards for the four key research terms given in Box 5.1 and four new cards for the glossary definitions. Pupils now have 14 pairs of Expert Researcher cards. They may like to make up a game of their own, play the games from earlier chapters or try out the new game given below.

Game 5: Fives

This game is best played with a group of three or four pupils. Shuffle the cards and give each player five cards and five counters. Leave the remaining cards in a pile face down on the table and put an empty tub next to this. The first player puts down one of her cards –which can be either a term or a definition –face up in the middle of the table and reads it out loud. The player to her left looks to see if she has the matching key term or matching definition. One of two actions happens:

1 If she does have a matching card she places this face up alongside the first card so that other players can check the accuracy. This matched pair is put to one side as these cards take no further part in the game. The player then chooses a second card from her hand to put face up on the table as a replacement (she now has only three cards in her hand) and play passes to the next player.

2 If she does not have a matching term or definition, she has to collect a card from the centre pile (she now has six cards in her hand) and has to pay one counter into the tub.

Play then passes to the next player who has to do the same. If players use up all their five counters before the game is complete they are knocked out and have to return all of their cards to the bottom of the centre pile. The winner is the first to get rid of all her cards without losing all five counters and she gets to keep all the counters in the tub. Multiple games can be played with pupils adding to their running tallies of counters.

Optional Extension Activity and Follow-up Work

Of course, the best way to develop observation research skills is to do it –lots of it, in both real and suspended time. There is an abundance of material suited to observation in suspended time. Some television documentaries such as the BBC series *Child of Our Time* provide excellent examples of behavioural situations which can be observed in structured and unstructured ways. Or you can create your own video data (with all the appropriate consents) to practise on.

Observation in real time can be set up within research teaching groups –pupils can observe each other, their teacher, their families and friends (again, ensuring that all the appropriate consents are obtained). Encourage pupils to undertake some unstructured observation and some systematic observation where they set up their own coding categories. They can practise their real-time observation skills in the playground and at home. Observing behaviour with pre-coded categories can be done from video footage and can give pupils experience in recording incidence and duration of behaviour. Do remember that if you are creating your own video for this purpose all the necessary consents must be obtained.

Key Reflection from Session 5

Observation is more than just looking, it is a key research tool and we can develop our observation skills through regular practice.

Suggested Further Reading

Christensen, P. and James, A. (2001) *Research with Children: Perspectives and Practices*, London: RoutledgeFalmer.

This is an edited volume of chapters relating to methodological issues of research with children and young people.

Interview Techniques

Learning aims	Knowledge content	Skills	Interactive elements	Pupil follow-up work	Curriculum links
To develop an appreciation of different interview structures and different question types	Framing questions Question bias Structured interviews and surveys Semi-structured interviews Unstructured interviews Group (focus) interviews	Open questioning Closed questioning Non-verbal body language Avoiding question bias	Individual and group interviews Expert Researcher card games	Interview practice	Literacy PSHE Citizenship

TEACHING CONTENT FOR SESSION 6

Timing: 90 minutes + 45 minutes follow-up work.

Introduction

The interview is a primary tool which is used a great deal, especially in qualitative research studies. Many researchers base their findings on data collected through interviews, others frequently use interviews as an additional method to give another dimension to their study to increase its relevance and validity. The interview can be used in many different ways and different question styles can be adopted to suit the purpose of the particular investigation. Skilful interviewing can help us to understand other people's feelings about important issues and find out more about their perceptions and interpretations of situations. In other words, interviewing can help us to determine people's values, preferences, attitudes and beliefs (Tuckman, 1972). However, there is a lot more to interviewing than simply asking a few questions and noting down the answers. In this book I concentrate on four types of interview:

- structured interviews
- semi-structured interviews
- unstructured interviews
- group interviews.

It is crucial that the style of interview is appropriate to the research question being posed. Interview styles vary according to the degree of structure researchers choose to adopt and this in turn is determined by the extent they want to be able to 'standardise' the data. If a researcher wants to collect data that can be compared across numerous individuals then the interview needs to be standardised. If a researcher is more interested in the uniqueness of the responses –in what individuals say about their particular situation then the interview needs to be more open-ended and unstructured to allow for maximum flexibility and individual responses. We will return to this theme again and also consider the issue of researcher bias when we have learned a little more about each different style of interview.

Structured Interviews

Structured interviews are used when a researcher is interested in standardised answers. They share some of the characteristics of a survey, although not generally on such a large scale and are administered verbally rather than as a written questionnaire. Let us suppose researchers are interested in children's views about school lunches. They might want to collect data about, for example, whether children think the portions are large enough, hot enough, healthy enough, sufficient choice, etc. These are straightforward questions and the answers lend themselves easily to standardisation and comparison across the pupil population. At the simplest level researchers could invite a yes or no response but this will not capture those answers where children's opinions are somewhere in between the two extremes of yes and no. Ideally, the question is framed in a way that allows some qualification of response but without this being too free, otherwise you end up with lots of different answers which are difficult to standardise. Limiting the choices available is one form of structure.

Staying with our example of school lunches, let us look at some possible phrasings of the first question about the size of portions and the likely outcomes.

Do you think the portions are big enough?

Do you think the portions are too small?

Do you think the portion size is generous?

Are you still hungry when you've finished your lunch?

Even though these all invite a yes or no response they are subtly different. By asking 'do you think the portions are *big* enough' the interviewer is subtly suggesting that the portions are big but are they big *enough?* By asking if they are *too small* the interviewer is planting in the interviewee's mind the idea that portions are small and asking if they think they are *too* small. Introducing the word *generous* has a similar affect and asking if the child is *still hungry* is planting an expectation in the respondents' minds that school lunches leave them hungry. This is what we call 'question-framing bias' and it often operates at a subconscious level when researchers are hardly aware they are being biased in the way they present a question. A much more neutrally phrased question would be,

What do you think about the size of the portions you get?

However, this is more open-ended and is likely to invite lots of different answers, e.g.:

They're okay.

Sometimes they're okay, like on Friday when we get chips
but sometimes it's pathetic.

I think they're quite generous.

Microscopic!

I don't know.

They're okay for me but I know my friend is always hungry.

They're about the same as I get at home.

They're not as big as I get at home.

They're okay if you can get seconds but there's no guarantee
there'll be any left over.

Pathetic!

I'm always starving.

It is difficult to standardise such wide-ranging answers. So, how do we resolve the dilemma of wanting to avoid oversimplicity in a yes/no response, avoid question-framing bias, and still be able to standardise the process? The way forward lies in giving interviewees a wider range of choice than yes/no but *limiting* this choice.

> Would you say that the portion size is about right, too small or too large?

If researchers asked this question to 100 Year 7 pupils, they could then compare the responses and draw conclusions, e.g.:

	Too large	About right	Too small
Number of pupils ($n = 100*$)	4	28	68

* n = is the shorthand terminology used to describe the total number of participants in a population sample.

The researcher might also be interested in whether there are any gender differences in the views being expressed.

	Too large		About right		Too small	
(Boys $n = 48$/girls $n = 52$)	boys	girls	boys	girls	boys	girls
	2	2	6	22	40	28

In a structured interview, a researcher could then do the same for each of the questions and collect data for comparison analysis. Our original example had four questions, so the other three might be phrased as:

> Are the hot lunches served at the right temperature, too hot or too cold?

> Do you think the lunches are very healthy, reasonably healthy or very unhealthy?

> Do you think the choice of food is good, adequate, poor or non-existent?

In very tightly structured interviews care is also taken to ensure interviewees receive the same questions, in the same order, with the same delivery (a researcher could ask the same question, but alter the emphasis on certain words or add emotional tone) in similar conditions. For example, the interview conditions might be for interviewees to be seated, one to one with the researcher and no adults present. If some interviews were then undertaken with teachers or lunchtime supervisors present, this might inhibit pupil responses and could affect the validity of the data. Interviewers commonly read their questions from a script. If this is so, you may wonder why the researcher does not simply give out a survey containing these questions and ask children to tick boxes.

Although the structured interview is quite similar, there are occasions when it would be better to administer the questions verbally than in a written form. This might be because some children may experience difficulties with reading or are too young to be able to read the questions for themselves or because the researcher wants to ensure that respondents clearly understand the questions and are not being influenced or coerced in any way when they answer. We will be looking at questionnaires and surveys later on but it is worth mentioning here that another reason researchers sometimes choose structured interviews over surveys is because the response rate of surveys is often very low.

Unstructured Interviews

Unstructured interviews are at the other end of the spectrum. This type of interview is open ended and designed to elicit individual and richly descriptive responses. It is used when a researcher wants to try and understand opinions and/or behaviour at a more complex level without pre-imposing any categories of response. Typically these are in-depth interviews which produce copious amounts of data. There are no set questions or predetermined frameworks for the responses. The role of the researcher is to gently probe when it is appropriate and to invite the interviewee to elaborate, qualify or clarify where necessary.

Let us consider how differently an unstructured interview about school lunches might unfold. A researcher might open with a very casual conversational-style question such as, 'What are the school lunches like here?' Indeed, an ethnographic researcher would very likely share the experience of an actual school lunch with an interviewee and approach the topic in a very casual way such as 'How's the lunch today?'. From this kind of initial foray, the researcher would hope to gather as much data as possible about the pupil's attitudes to, views about and emotional interaction with school lunches. Occasionally the researcher will seek clarification or elaboration or steer the conversation towards a particular area, e.g. the social aspects of school lunch or the healthy living element, but in the main an unstructured interview is driven by the responses given.

Semi-structured Interviews

Somewhere in between these two models is the semi-structured interview and this type of interview is increasingly being adopted. Researchers have a small core of predetermined questions or topic areas which they want to ask but beyond that the interview is unstructured and unscripted. The core questions are not necessarily asked in any specific order and may not even need to be asked directly if the answers crop up in general conversation. The most important characteristic of a semi-structured interview is flexibility. This allows the interviewer freedom to pick up on individual responses and take the questioning in different directions where appropriate.

Let us focus on an example from our school lunch scenario. The four initial topic areas of portion size, temperature, healthy eating and choice might easily form core themes which the researchers want to ensure are covered and they will field a direct question if these areas do not come up in conversation. A semi-structured interview might typically begin,

Interviewer (I):   What are the school lunches like here?

Respondent (R): They're awful. I wanted to stop having them and bring a packed lunch but my mum won't let me.

Already, a researcher has an interesting trail which may be pursued or let go. Choice was one of the pre-established themes for this interview but this was in relation to the food choice and here, already is an interesting situation about who exercises power and control over the choice of school or packed lunches. A researcher could turn away from this trail by following up with,

I: Why do you say they're awful?

Or, the researcher could pick up on the response and probe more deeply with questions such as,

I: Why do you think your mum won't let you have packed lunches?

This in turn, could lead on to other response trails such as having to have free school meals or parents thinking children get a 'good, hot dinner' etc.

I: Do you think parents or children should make the decision about whether you have school or packed lunches?

This kind of question could lead on to others about power issues etc.

A considerable degree of skill is required on the part of the researcher to steer the interview in search of richly descriptive data without allowing the interview to wander so far from core themes as to become completely unstructured. If this happens, it becomes more difficult for the researcher to analyse data in a thematic way later on.

Group Interviews

Here, the researcher works with several people at the same time rather than interviewing individuals and the group interview (sometimes called a 'focus' interview) can be structured, semi-structured or unstructured. The role of the researcher is different in a group interview and the process is less like an interview and more like a 'steered discussion'. The researcher is more of a facilitator and is interested in group interaction as well as the statements being made. The researcher guides the topic of the discussion and, depending on the degree of structure required, the questions. One advantage of asking questions in groups is this can sometimes access information which might not be as forthcoming in individual interviews.

Let us think about a scenario from our school lunch topic. A researcher has gathered together eight participants, four girls and four boys from a Year 9 class, to discuss school lunches. In answer to the researcher's question, 'What about the time you get to eat your lunch?', the following discussion ensued:

Girl 1:   I'd say about 15 minutes.

Girl 2:   You're lucky, then –you must get near the front of the queue. I usually have to throw mine down in five minutes, 'cos by the time I get there the queue's a mile long! I always seem to have PE or Art or something like that just before lunch and we never get out on time.

Boy 2:   Yeah, I'm generally at the back of the queue as well and I don't think it's fair that the Prefects come and push in ahead of us.

Girl 4:   And loads of people use fake early lunch passes, Darren Clark's got a right scam going there.

Boy 4:   My sister always manages to get near the front of the queue …

Boy 3:   That's because she's in Year 7, they always let the babies go first it's not fair, *and* they get bigger portions than us, even though they're younger cos by the time we get there they're cutting the pizza slices a lot smaller *and* theirs is hotter.

Girl 3:   I think there should be a much fairer system. We should all get a proper turn at being near the front of the queue.

At this point the researcher could let the conversation carry on in this vein and collect some valuable data about power issues which might not have come up in individual interviews or choose to steer it in a different direction, or even steer back to something that was buried in the flurry of statements. This particular researcher chose to wind back to Boy 3's comment about those getting in earliest getting the largest portions even though they might be younger.

Interviewer:	Do you think any distinction should be made about size of portion according to age or size or gender?
Girl 2:	Everybody knows that boys eat more than girls.
Girl 1:	I don't think that's always true, I know loads of girls who eat more than boys –it depends on your appetite …
Boy 1:	And your age …
Boy 3:	It's not just your age it's your size too …
Girl 4:	Yeah, and it's all about metabolic rate and stuff …
Boy 2:	Yeah, if you've just had PE and been running round a football pitch for half an hour you're likely to be more hungry than if you've been doing Spanish conversation.
Girl 3:	But that would be impossible to sort out –how would the dinner ladies know who's had PE and who hasn't!
Boy 4:	Why can't we have a system where we can just have as much as we want, then it wouldn't matter how old you are, or what size you are or if you're a girl or a boy, everyone would have what's right for them.
Girl 1:	But some kids might be greedy and take more than they need …

The researcher's role is to steer and moderate the discussion so that it does not go too far off at a tangent but has enough flexibility to explore interesting trails. Sometimes there can be problems with group discussions. The group dynamics may not work and one child might end up dominating the discussion or perhaps differences of opinion become heated or one member of the group is singled out for ridicule. Again, it is down to the skill of the researcher to know when to intervene and when to draw a session to a close.

Researchers are not confined to just one type of interview, they may opt to use more than one. Sometimes a researcher carries out initial structured interviews and then follows these up with some selected semi-structured interviews with certain participants. The group interview is also used as a preparatory tool as well as a data collection tool, e.g. by undertaking a group interview a researcher might come to know what thematic areas she or he wants to concentrate on when designing a questionnaire or a structured interview. Interviews are also commonly used alongside other research methods such as observation and experiment.

Practical Issues about Interviewing

There are many issues to think about when preparing for an interview. First and foremost are the ethics. Here are some guidelines for pupils:

- You must always seek informed consent (see Chapter 3) before carrying out an interview and explain to the interviewee what your purpose is and what you intend to do with the data you collect, and come to an agreement about the extent of confidentiality. If you are interviewing schoolchildren you will also need consent from parents and, if this is done during school hours, permission from teachers.

- Think about the location where you will carry out the interview. If this is in school, will the school context, and all the rules and constraints that this incorporates, affect the likely responses? If you interview a child at home, are there likely to be similar constraints in the home environment?

- How will you put your interviewees at ease and gain their trust?

- How will you record the data, by handwritten notes, audio- or video-taping?

- Estimate how long you think the interview will take and allow plenty of time.

- Consider whether a child might prefer to be interviewed with a friend?

- How many children will you interview and on what basis will you choose them (e.g. age, gender, etc).

- Do you need to practise first or to pilot your questions?

- Do be aware that a lot of communication is non-verbal and your facial and bodily expressions may convey signs of approval, disapproval, enthusiasm or boredom, which could affect the nature of the responses. Even just a slight fidgeting movement in your chair might give the impression that you are bored. Practise adopting a neutral but interested and active listening pose.

- Show that you are actively listening –listening is different from hearing –you can show this by alluding to past statements and making your comments relevant to what has been said.

- Avoid interrupting your interviewee as this can give the impression that you are not interested in what they have to say.

- Always remember to thank the participant for the interview and to indicate that you enjoyed talking to them and value their views.

BOX 6.1   KEY RESEARCH TERMS FOR SESSION 6

focus group interview: a group interview with a focused theme where interpersonal dynamics and the interaction of participants in respect of one another's comments forms an important element in the data.

semi-structured interview: an interview based on a core of key questions with the additional flexibility of following up responses with further, more individualised questions.

structured interview: a tightly framed interview consisting of a series of closed questions which are repeated in exactly the same way to all interviewees.

unstructured interview: an interview with no predetermined questions based more loosely on conversational-style questions around the general topic area.

Core Activity

You will need to use the three interview transcripts from Photocopiable Resource 6 for this activity. Print out sufficient for a set of interview transcripts between two pupils.

Intermediate level

In pairs, pupils read the three transcripts and decide whether these are structured, semi-structured or unstructured interviews and give their reasons. Then, they examine the transcripts more closely and try to identify different styles of questions. Pupils should mark these with a letter code as follows:

- open questions (O)
- closed questions (C)
- follow-up questions (F)
- leading questions (L)
- key questions (K)

Simpler level

Work only from the structured interview (Interview 1 with Rashid)

Advanced level

Pupils could also look for bias (B) and value judgements (V).

Expert Researcher Card Games

Make new cards for the four key research terms and glossary definitions given in Box 6.1. Pupils now have 18 pairs of Expert Researcher cards. They may like to make up a game of their own, play the games described in earlier chapters or try out the new game described below.

Game 6: Experts

This game can be played in small groups plus one 'adjudicator' who could be the teacher or an experienced group leader. Use the 18 playing cards with the key research terms on them. You will not need the cards with the glossary definitions on for this game. However, the teacher/facilitator will need to use the Collated Glossary, which contains the correct definitions (see Photocopiable Resource 12). In addition make 18 round tokens with the words *RESEARCH EXPERT* written on each one.

Shuffle the playing cards and place them in a pile face down on the table. One by one, each player turns over a card from the central pack and has to attempt a definition. If the definition is judged by the leader to be completely accurate then that playing card is set aside and the player is given a *RESEARCH EXPERT* token. If not, the playing card is returned to the bottom of the pack. Players continue in their turn to attempt to be research experts until all the cards have been accurately defined and all the *RESEARCH EXPERT* tokens given out. The winner is the player with the most tokens.

Optional Extension Activity and Follow-up Work

Obviously, the best possible activity for children to engage in is practising real interviews for themselves. Initially, this can be done with one another in pairs and in small groups. Once confident, they could practise on family and friends (with all the appropriate permissions and consents, of course). It is a good idea to audio- or video-record these attempts so that pupils can evaluate their own performances. It is also a good idea to look out for examples of interviews on television and radio programmes and encourage pupils to discuss their relative merits and characteristics, e.g. what degree of structure they have. BBC Radio 4 programmes such as *You and Yours* and *The Learning Curve* often have interesting semi-structured interviews.

Key Reflection from Session 6

Skilful interviewing can help us to understand other people's feelings about important issues and find out more about their perceptions and interpretations of situations.

Suggested Further Reading

Clark, A., and Moss, P. (2001) *Listening to Young Children: The Mosaic Approach*, London: National Children's Bureau.

Lewis, A. (2002) Accessing, through research interviews, the views of children with difficulties in learning, *Support for Learning*, 17(3): 110–115.

Questionnaires and Surveys

Learning aims	Knowledge content	Skills	Interactive elements	Pupil follow-up work	Curriculum links
To develop an understanding of good and poor questionnaire design	Likert-type scales Questioning bias Population samples	Framing open and closed questions Recognising question bias Constructing attitudinal measuring scales	Group discussion Attitude scale exercise Questionnaire design Expert Researcher card games	Design a mini questionnaire	Citizenship PSHE Geography Maths Literacy RS

TEACHING CONTENT FOR SESSION 7

Timing: 2 hours + 1 hour follow-up work.

Introduction

In some ways the questionnaire can be seen as a structured interview in written form. It is a popular method of data collection because it can be distributed to larger numbers and, since the answers are standardised, the analysis is relatively straightforward (Wilson and McLean, 1994). Many questionnaires are anonymous, and this generally increases the likelihood of people responding honestly to the questions. However, there are some drawbacks. Questionnaires which are sent out by post frequently have a low response rate – sometimes as low as 20 per cent –and this has validity implications because there is then an issue about how 'representative' the data can be from such a small percentage of a population sample. Also, the written questionnaire is dependent on participants being able to read and, unless steps are taken to support people with reading difficulties, English as a second language or visual disabilities, then the method might be interpreted as exclusionary.

The questionnaire is an effective tool for determining factual information, e.g.:

- Are you male or female?
- Are you aged 5-8 years, 9-12 years or 13-16?
- Do you come to school ..by car, bus, train, cycle, on foot?

Questionnaires are also used to explore people's views, opinions and attitudes although it is less easy to determine nuances of opinions and attitudes in a questionnaire than in an unstructured interview. If attitudes are being sought then skilful use of scaling needs to be employed. This brings us back to one of the recurring themes of this book, the importance of a data collection method being appropriate to the research question. Hence the way we design a questionnaire has to be driven by the research question. Generally speaking, the larger the sample size the more structured and closed the questions need to be. In the remainder of this chapter we are going to explore different approaches to questionnaire design and look at some practical examples.

Question Types

Most questionnaires require at least some factual questions. It may be important to your research question to know the respondents' age, gender, type of school, number of siblings, etc. Factual questions require a simple yes/no answer or a choice from a 'category' answer. Here are some examples.

Tick ONE box only.

Are you   female ☐   male ☐

Are you in   Year 6 ☐   Year 7 ☐   Year 8 ☐

How many siblings do you have? 1 ☐ 2 ☐ 3 ☐ more than 3 ☐

Many researchers use questionnaires to find out what people's views and attitudes are about a subject. Supposing they are researching children's views about school uniform, simple yes/no answers may provide factual information but they give little indication of strength of opinion. However, if a researcher were to interview everyone individually to try and determine the strength of their views it might take too long, or perhaps the children live too far away and can only be reached by post (e.g. a comparison between attitudes to school uniform in England and Scotland, or between a state school and an independent school). Also, such individual interviews can result in a vast range of answers which are then difficult for the researcher to 'standardise' for analysis.

In an interview situation it is possible to clarify any misunderstanding about a question at the time of asking. With a written questionnaire there is no such opportunity, so care needs to be taken to ensure that every question is crystal clear and unambiguous. The last of the factual questions shown above – *How many siblings do you have?* –appears straightforward, but is actually quite ambiguous because some children who have half-brothers and half-sisters or step-brothers and step-sisters will not know whether to include them in their response. Equally, children may have adult siblings or half-siblings who live somewhere else and this could be significant to the research question posed and the data being collected. To avoid misunderstandings, pose such a question as, *How many siblings (including half-siblings and step-siblings) live with you in your home?*

Testing Attitudes

Many questionnaires seek to find out more about people's attitudes to a certain issue. In this situation, the questionnaire is often framed as a set of statements where respondents are invited to select a category which most closely matches their own viewpoint. For example, researchers investigating children's attitudes to school councils might prepare statements like:

> School councils are a good idea.
>
> Elections for pupil representatives to school councils are just a popularity contest.
>
> Our school council representative never tells us anything about what's going on so we might as well not have one.
>
> Pupils generally vote for someone sensible to be their school council representative.
>
> Adults never listen to what children have to say at school council meetings.
>
> School councils are a waste of time.

Once the statements are prepared, the researchers then decide what degree of scale to use, according to how deeply they want to test attitudes. The simplest scale is *Agree/Disagree* or *Agree/Disagree/Don't know*. While these give a broad overview of opinion they do not test the strength of opinion. If, in response to the statement, *school councils are a waste of time*, 97 children out of 100 decide to tick *Agree* and the remaining three decide to tick *Disagree*, you would be tempted to conclude that there was overwhelming dissatisfaction with school councils. Without a middle, 'sit on the fence' category, individuals are encouraged to choose agreement or disagreement about a statement they may not have a firm opinion on either way. If, a *not sure* category is added, the picture may look somewhat different.

Agree	Neither agree nor disagree	Disagree
70	28	2

When respondents are offered a wider choice, the picture may change even more, as is shown by the answers given by the same 100 participants responding to the same statement with the following categories: *Strongly agree/Agree/Neither agree nor disagree/Disagree/Strongly disagree.*

Strongly agree	Agree	Neither agree nor disagree	Disagree	Strongly disagree
7	63	28	1	1

When the choice of category is increased to seven, the researcher gets closer to the reality of children's views

Strongly agree	Agree	Slightly agree	Neither agree nor disagree	Slightly disagree	Disagree	Strongly disagree
7	50	28	1	13	0	1

Let us look at how the same 100 children's attitudes to the statement, *School councils are a waste of time*, are represented differently according to the scale used. Look particularly at what happens to the *agree* category and the *disagree* categories.

Strongly agree	Agree	Slightly agree	Neither agree nor disagree	Slightly disagree	Disagree	Strongly disagree
-	97	-	-	-	3	-
-	70	-	28	-	2	-
7	63	-	28	-	1	1
7	50	28	1	13	0	1

Although 97 of the 100 children agreed that 'school councils are a waste of time', it turned out that only seven of those felt strongly about this, and when given the choice to neither agree nor disagree, 27 of those 97, opted for this (plus one of the three who chose to disagree originally). However, when the additional category of slightly agree or disagree was added, most of the children felt they could now come 'off the fence' because slight agreement or disagreement was much closer to how they really felt about school councils being a waste of time.

These kinds of scale which use a range of categories to measure attitudes are frequently known as *Likert scales*, named after the researcher who first designed them (Likert, 1932). Likert-type scales can be used to provide numerical data. For example, our question about school councils being a waste of time could be expressed as,

To what extent do you agree or disagree with the following statements? Circle a number from 0 to 10 where 10 represents very strong agreement and 0 very strong disagreement:

School councils are a waste of time   10   9   8   7   6   5   4   3   2   1   0

Likert-type scales can also be adapted for younger children, using a series of facial expressions and inviting young children to choose the face that best expresses their viewpoint.

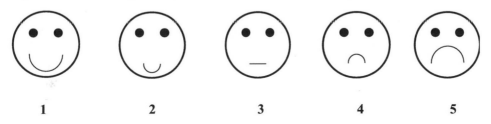

1   2   3   4   5

Choose the face that best describes how you feel about

Drawing pictures

Playing out in the snow

Story time

Creating a measurement scale does not always have to involve degrees of agreement or disagreement (although these are certainly easier to code and analyse). You can create a bank of responses to each question e.g.:

School councils are

a)   a waste of time

b)   a good idea

c)   ineffective

d)   unrealistic

e)   brilliant

f)   corrupt

or

How important is it to feel liked by your teacher?

1   not at all important

2   a little important

3   quite important

4   important

5   very important

Adapted questionnaires with facial expression do not always have to be based on degrees of 'smiling'. Faces could feature expressions of anger, boredom, happiness, frustration, sadness, anxiety, etc.

Question Bias

It is important to avoid bias in the way the questions are phrased. Researchers probably have a personal opinion about the topic they are exploring and, even though they want to keep an open mind and undertake a valid study, it can still be difficult to prevent personal views colouring the nature of their questions. Let us stay with the school council example above. The six questions shown are only a small part of the design, but if those six questions formed the entire questionnaire then it could be argued that they demonstrate researcher bias. There are five negative statements about school councils and one positive statement. Even though respondents have the opportunity to disagree with the statements, and thus display a positive attitude, the overall tone of the questions is negative. This can have a subconscious effect on the respondents who are completing the questionnaire and may lead them to adopt slightly more negative views than might have been the case if the questions had been more neutral. It may be that the researcher has a negative attitude to school councils and is subconsciously seeking to have her or his own viewpoint upheld in the data.

Compare these question examples from two different questionnaires both about school councils. They both use the same seven-point Likert scale of strongly agree, agree, slightly agree, neither agree nor disagree, slightly disagree, disagree, strongly disagree.

Extract from Questionnaire A

School councils are a good idea.

Our school council pupil representative does a good job.

Adults are very respectful of pupils' views expressed at school council meetings.

We have a good ratio of pupils to adults on our school council.

Extract from Questionnaire B

School councils are a waste of time.

Elections for pupil representatives to school councils are just a popularity contest.

Adults never listen to what children have to say at school council meetings.

The ratio of pupils to adults on our school council is very poor.

At a subconscious level the tone of these questions may have an effect on the answers of some respondents. However, if the statements were made excessively bland, such as 'School councils are okay', they would not succeed in probing depth of opinion, so bold statements should not necessarily be ruled out. What researchers often do to try and balance their questionnaire and prevent bias of this kind is to ask the same question in both a negative and a positive way, preferably not consecutively but spaced several questions apart. So a questionnaire about school councils may well have all eight of the questions listed above in the same document.

A much more blatant bias is when the question is 'loaded' with value judgements which suggest that there is only one acceptable answer e.g.:

In Geography do you prefer learning about rocks, fossils and other old things or useful information about the environment we live in today that can help us make the world a better place?

Ethical Issues

There are several ethical issues to consider. Any investigative process relating to people's lives, especially their feelings and emotions, has the potential to cause harm or distress, so questions and statements need to be designed carefully. The topic area may be a sensitive one such as bullying and, if respondents have had personal experience of bullying either as victims or perpetrators, then the questions may resurrect some painful memories. Assurance of anonymity and confidentiality are other important steps to prevent anxiety or potential distress. Another area where possible harm might ensue is the way in which researchers use the data they collect from questionnaires. The data themselves should not be used in a way that causes harm to any individual. Therefore researchers should always include a preliminary statement before the questions explaining what the questionnaire is about, what the purpose of the research is and how the data will be used. An illustrative example is set out below.

> I am doing some research about children's attitudes to school uniform. The information collected from this questionnaire will be analysed to explore any significant differences in children's attitudes according to their age and gender. The questionnaire is anonymous and all the information collected will be treated confidentially. As age and gender are an important factor in the investigation, please could you ensure you tick the age and gender boxes that apply to you. Thank you very much for your help.
>
> Leslie Vernon, aged 12, pupil researcher.

Designing Questionnaires

The skill in designing a questionnaire is the ability to funnel down from a general topic to a concrete, focused aspect of the subject which will enable pupils to gather useful data. In other words, they need to define what the primary objective of their questionnaire is going to be and then identify secondary areas which link into this and which can form the basis of questions.

Step 1:   General area of interest → school councils (too large and vague) →

Step 2: Pupils' views about school councils (more focused and manageable) →

Step 3: Specific aspects of pupils' views that I want to find out more about → pupil election process; adult-pupil power relations; ratio of adults to pupils; feedback from pupil representative (plus do I need to consider gender issues here?) →

Step 4: Design some questions/statements around each specific
aspect →

Step 5: Decide on a measurement scale.

Unstructured questionnaires

Not all questionnaires are as structured as the examples given so far; some can
be more exploratory and pose open-ended questions. This enables the respondents to answer in a more personal way and to represent their views without
constraint and without ambiguity. This, of course, is only possible if the sample size is relatively small because the analysis is more involved and sometimes this can take just as long as the analysis of an unstructured interview.

Open-ended questions can be framed in different ways. As a question,
you might ask:

What do you think is the most beneficial thing about school councils?

....

....

What do you like least about school councils?

....

....

What do you think about school councils?

....

....

Or sentence completion such as,

School councils are ....

....

....

An effective pupil representative is ....

....

....

Ordering the questions

I have already mentioned that researchers sometimes ask the same question in opposite ways to avoid bias and also to check consistency of response and that when doing this a researcher tries to space these out. There are a few other considerations to think about when you are deciding on the sequencing of your questions. In general, it is best to start with easy, straightforward, factual questions, then move on to closed questions which elicit opinions through multiple choice routes, and leave any open-ended questions which require fuller, more personal answers towards the end. Questions of a sensitive or contentious nature are also generally best left towards the end. There are exceptions, of course; some simple, straightforward factual questions may become sensitive ones in certain circumstances. *How many grandparents do you have?* might appear straightforward but could be sensitive to someone whose grandmother has just died. So there can never be any absolute rules, just general guidance and a lot of common sense. Box 7.1 contains ten tips for questionnaire design.

BOX 7.1 TOP TEN TIPS FOR QUESTIONNAIRE DESIGN

1 Include an introductory paragraph that explains your research.
2 Invite people to contact you for more information if they wish.
3 Give clear instructions on how to return the questionnaire.
4 Include a return-by date.
5 Make questions unambiguous.
6 Avoid leading questions.
7 Avoid 'loaded' questions.
8 Keep language as simple as possible.
9 Avoid long-winded questions that ramble.
10 Avoid phrasing questions with negatives (especially avoid double negatives).

Core Activity

The core activity is intended to demonstrate to pupils, at first hand, the effect that different measurement scales have on the outcome of responses. This activity is best carried out with a minimum number of 16 children.

Prepare a simple set of statements about a topic which you feel confident the pupils you are working with will have an opinion about. An obvious choice would be a subject like school uniform because all pupils, whether they have to wear it or not, are likely to have an opinion about it. A sample of six questions is plenty, otherwise it will take too long to process the responses. Write the same set of statements out four times, each time using a different response scale and ask the pupils to complete each of the four short questionnaires in turn. You can use Photocopiable Resource 7 for this activity or create a design of your own.

When pupils have completed all four questionnaires get them to tally the answers and compare how differently the strength of opinion changes according to what scale is employed. Discuss the implications of this with regard to design issues and outcome effects.

Here is an example of what happened in a live exercise with a group of Year 7 pupils who used Photocopiable Resource 7. The example illustrates what happened to their responses to question 5 'Children should only wear school uniform from Year 3 upwards' in Questionnaire 1 when 16 pupils completed the four different ranking scales.

	Agree	Disagree
5. Children should only wear school uniform from Year 3 upwards	9	7

	Agree	Neither agree nor disagree	Disagree
5. Children should only wear school uniform from Year 3 upwards	6	6	4

	Strongly agree	Agree	Neither agree nor disagree	Disagree	Strongly disagree
5. Children should only wear school uniform from Year 3 upwards	2	4	6	2	2

	Strongly agree	Agree	Slightly agree	Neither agree nor disagree	Slightly disagree	Disagree	Strongly disagree
5. Children should only wear school uniform from Year 3 upwards	2	1	5	2	3	1	2

Follow-up Work

There are many activities you can do with pupils around the design elements of questionnaires. Create a set of questions or statements around a given topic and get pupils to decide about the kind of question or statement posed, e.g. is it a 'leading' question, a 'closed' question, an open question, a 'loaded' question? Then pupils, working in pairs or small groups, can see if they can compose an example of each of these. There can be no substitute for actually having a go and, undoubtedly, the best way to develop these research skills is to practise designing questionnaires. Begin with a research topic, e.g. *Investigating children's views about pocket money*. Start with simple designs and only a few questions or statements. Think about what you want to find out, what kinds of questions will help you to access that information and how finely graded you need the responses to be. How will you analyse the responses? Do you want to do any comparisons? Let pupils critique one another's designs and suggest improvements.

Expert Researcher Card Games

Make cards for the four new key research terms and their glossary definitions as they appear in Box 7.2. You will also need to make seven small cards bearing the word 'expert researcher life' and make compilation glossaries available to pupils so that they can check the accuracy of their moves (use Photocopiable Resource 12).

BOX 7.2 KEY RESEARCH TERMS FOR SESSION 7

closed question: a question which restricts the responses that can be made by having a predetermined set of possible answers.

Likert scale: a five-point scale used to measure responses in a range such as 'very good/good/neutral/poor/very poor'.

open question: a question which does not limit the response that can be given nor suggest the kind of answer a researcher might be looking for.

population sample: a group of people who participate in research, the choice of people can be predetermined or random according to what is appropriate for the research question. The number of the population sample similarly varies according to the research question. Generally, quantitative methods have the larger population samples.

Game 7: Solo sevens

All the games so far in this book have been designed for pairs or small groups. Game 7 in the Expert Researcher card games is for individual players.

Shuffle the cards and place seven cards face up in a row in the middle of a table. Deal seven cards to yourself. Place the rest of the cards in a pile face down on the table and next to them put the seven 'expert researcher life' cards. Look at the cards in your hand and those face up on the table and see if you can match up any pairs (check in the Glossary – Photocopiable Resource 12 – if you are unsure of any definitions). If you can match any pairs then you stack the pairs and replace them with new cards for each pair from the pile (these are placed one in your hand and one on the table, irrespective of where the paired cards came from originally). If you cannot match a pair you must use up one of your 'expert researcher lives' to 'buy' a pair of cards from the pile. Put one card in your hand and the other on the table. Check to see if you can now match a pair. If so, stack the pair and replace them with two cards from the central pile as before. If you still cannot match a pair from your hand with one of the cards on the table you must use up a second 'life' to buy another pair. Play continues like this until all the pairs are matched or you run out of 'lives'. If you run out of lives you have lost. If you get a completion, note how many lives you used and try and beat this next time you play.

Optional Extension Activity

Pupils can explore how other researchers have used questionnaires in their research studies. Some good examples can be found in the edited volume of research papers in the suggested further reading at the end of Chapter 2 (Lewis, V., Kellett, M., Robinson, C., Fraser, S. and Ding, S. (eds) (2004) *The Reality of Research with Children and Young People*, London: Sage in association with OUP). Alternatively several of the research studies featured on the Children's Research Centre website use questionnaires in their methodology: http://childrens-research-centre.open.ac.uk.

Key Reflection from Session 7

A great deal of thought and planning goes into the design of a questionnaire in order to avoid bias and to ensure participants have sufficient response choices to express their viewpoints accurately.

Suggested Further Reading

Scott, J. (2000) Children as respondents: the challenge for quantitative methods, in P. Christensen and A. James (eds), *Research with Children: Perspectives and Practices*, London: RoutledgeFalmer, pp. 98–117.

CHAPTER 8

Experimental Techniques

Learning aims	Knowledge content	Skills	Interactive elements	Pupil follow-up work	Curriculum links
To appreciate how to design a valid research experiment	Validity	Hypothesis formulation	Group discussion	Experimental design exercise	Science
To understand how to formulate hypotheses	Independent and dependent variables	Control and manipulation of variables	Experimental design activities		
To begin to develop an understanding of variables in experimental research	Extraneous variables		Expert Researcher card games		

TEACHING CONTENT FOR SESSION 8

Timing: 90 minutes + 30 minutes follow-up work.

Introduction

Experimental techniques in research share some similarities to methods taught in school science teaching. In simple terms, experimental methods are concerned with *cause and effect*, with being able to *measure* the extent of an effect and attribute a likely cause. This is done by the control and manipulation of what we call *variables*. In a pure experimental design a researcher wants to isolate a variable so that its effect can be measured or tested. Let us take a very simple example from the kind of activity pupils might be engaged in at school.

Supposing we want to find out if a new 'miracle' fertiliser, which has just come on the market, promotes faster-growing tomatoes. We might take a batch of tomato plants and divide them in half so that we can treat one half with the new miracle fertiliser and the other half with normal fertiliser, and then compare the results. But there are lots of other 'variables' which can affect plant growth –e.g. sunlight, water, quality of the soil, etc. –and we need to know whether or not it is the miracle fertiliser which is the *cause* of the fast growth *effect*. Therefore, we have to try and 'neutralise' all other possible causes, what researchers call *extraneous* variables. To do this researchers set up an experimental situation where all conditions other than one are the same. For example, they would put the plants in the same soil type, in the same position, so that they get the same amount of sunlight and give them the same amount of water each day. This is called 'controlling the variables'. The one condition which remains different is the fertiliser, and this is known as the *independent variable*. After a period of time the researcher measures the outcome, in other words the *effect* on tomato plant growth. This effect is the *dependent variable*. If the tomatoes which have been fed the 'miracle' fertiliser have grown faster than the others then, because the researcher kept all other conditions the same, the likely cause of this enhanced growth can be attributed to the new fertiliser. These variables can be summarised as follows:

- independent variable = the 'miracle' fertiliser
- dependent variable = the plant growth
- extraneous variables = soil type, amount of sunlight, amount of water.

This kind of research design is a controlled group comparison. Of course, it is a lot easier to set up a controlled experiment for tomato plants than it is for human beings. The situation is much more complex with people and there are lots of ethical issues to consider.

Population Samples

One of the factors which helps give the tomato experiment validity is that the plants come from the same 'batch', and for all intents and purposes could be considered to be the same. When we do experimental research involving people it is a lot harder to find people who are 'the same', or from the same 'batch', as it were.

Supposing researchers want to investigate whether pollution affects tomato plant growth, they could set up a similar experiment where the independent variable would be the level of pollution. However, if researchers wanted to investigate whether pollution affects children's reading ability, it is not quite so straightforward. Supposing they found an urban school surrounded by busy roads and heavy traffic, and compared this with a rural school in a sleepy village. The researchers give 20 children in each school a reading test and then compare the results. Why would this not be a valid group comparison? To a point, the researchers have isolated pollution as an independent variable but the rest of the design is seriously flawed. First, 20 is much too small a number to decide whether pollution has any significant effect on reading ability –such a study would need to look at a sample of thousands. Secondly, the two groups are not adequately 'matched' for other factors which can affect reading ability such as age, reading experience, levels of home reading support, expertise of the teachers, etc.

Pre-test/Post-test Design

Another experimental method sometimes used is referred to as a pre-test/post-test design. This relates to measuring the effect of an intervention. Participants are tested first (the pre-test) to provide baseline data. An intervention approach is introduced and then participants are tested again at the end of the intervention period (post-test). Supposing researchers want to find out whether pupils' spelling ability improves with a new teaching approach. Using a standardised spelling test, they could assess the spelling ability of a group of children and record the scores. This is the pre-test and provides baseline data. Then the new spelling approach is introduced. After an agreed length of time (e.g. half a term) the researchers re-test the pupils using a similarly standardised test (the post-test) and compare the new scores for each pupil. To control the variables the researchers would have to ensure that the pupils were not receiving any other kind of tuition elsewhere (at home for instance) and that they were exposed to similar amounts of the intervention approach in school (e.g. some pupils may have been absent for an extended period of time). The researchers would also have to allow for what we call 'natural maturation', this means the level at which spelling would be expected to improve from having half a term of schooling and being half a term older. Age-standardised tests would help to control this variable. One-off pre-test/post-test designs are sometimes criticised for being too simplistic and are often used in conjunction with other methods –e.g. observation and/or interview –so that information is provided from more than one source. This process is called *triangulation*.

Withdrawal Design

When testing the effect of an intervention approach a withdrawal technique might be used. This design involves introducing an approach, measuring its effect and then withdrawing the approach to see if the effect is halted or reversed. For example, if researchers want to investigate the extent to which a fish oil supplement affects children's ability to concentrate, they might give a group of children a daily fish oil supplement and observe and/or measure their concentration levels for a set period of time. After this period the fish oil supplement is withdrawn to see if concentration levels revert back to pre-intervention levels. However, there are ethical implications in some designs which incorporate a withdrawal phase. If you hypothesise that an intervention may have a beneficial effect, possibly even a life-transforming quality, it would be unethical to withdraw the intervention – and by implication, the improved quality of life –in order to prove it.

Core Activity

Three experimental scenarios are provided in Photocopiable Resource 8. They are differentiated for ability level, 8a being the simpler of the three, 8b intermediate level and 8c more advanced. Choose an appropriate scenario to discuss in a small group situation. Ask pupils to identify the independent, dependent and extraneous variables and to discuss what a researcher would need to do in order to set up a valid experiment. Consider what the ethical implications might be.

Guided comment: simpler level scenario – drinking water experiment

In this experiment, the independent variable is the water and the dependent variable is the effect the water has on pupil concentration. Extraneous variables which need to be accounted for include:

- How will the researcher 'measure' the dependent variable, i.e. measure the effect of drinking water during the day?

- Just giving access to water does not necessarily mean that pupils will drink water, so how do you know if they have drunk any more than the comparison group? How do you control for this?

Has the researcher thought about the ethical implications of *requiring* pupils to drink a certain amount of water? What are the ethical implications of preventing pupils from drinking water during the school day? Have all the implications been fully explained when seeking consent? Is the researcher going to control other amounts of fluid available to either group or is it just the amount of water the researcher is interested in? How will levels of pupil concentration be measured?

Guided comment: intermediate level scenario – growth drug experiment

The independent variable is the growth drug and the dependent variable is the increase in height. A researcher might use a control group experiment, giving the growth drug to one group but not the other. It would be important to 'match' the two groups in terms of medical diagnosis, age, height, annual growth rates, etc. The ethical implications are extensive, e.g.:

- Should a drug of this nature be tested on human beings?
- Would it be ethical to test a drug like this on animals?
- Can researchers be confident there will be no detrimental side effects?
- Will it raise unrealistic expectations for participants and will there be emotional trauma if the drug does not work?
- Full, informed consent is imperative.

Guided comment: advanced level scenario – baby colour preference experiment

Here, the independent variable is colour and the dependent variable is the amount of play time given to each colour. There are several extraneous variables to control for. Some examples are:

- the teddies must be the same in all but colour, that is one must not have a more interesting face than another or be a different size or made of different material
- the positioning of the teddies –whether or not one is more readily visible or readily accessible than another
- the researcher needs to decide what to do in the event of a baby throwing one (or all) of the teddies out of the play pen.

The ethical considerations revolve around the emotional well-being of the baby. What should the researcher do if the baby becomes distressed? If video is to be used, what will become of the data? What does the researcher need to do to ensure informed consent is gained?

BOX 8.1 KEY RESEARCH TERMS FOR SESSION 8

dependent variable: the variable which shows the effect of an influence.

independent variable: the variable which exerts an influence.

triangulation: a process which uses more than one method of data collection in order to increase the validity of the research data.

variable: something which can have two or more levels of difference, e.g. gender can be one of two variables – male or female – and hair colour can be one of several variables.

Follow-up Work

Having discussed one or more of the given experimental scenarios, pupils can follow this up by writing out a detailed plan of an experimental method for one of the scenarios.

Expert Researcher Card Games

Make cards for the new key research terms and definitions shown in Box 8.1. This game requires the invention of false definitions of the key research terms. Depending on the age and ability of pupils these can be close aberrations of the correct definition, more obviously erroneous definitions or for a fun activity these can be 'whacky' or spoof definitions.

Game 8: Call my bluff

Pupils play this in teams of three plus one 'game host'. Choose 20 key research terms for this game and allocate ten to each team. The teams must then invent two false definitions for each term in secret (teachers can invent these in advance if preferred). When both teams are prepared they come together for the contest. The game host reads out the first of the ten key research terms given to team A. The players in team A then present three definitions, only one of which is the true one and team B have to decide who is telling the truth. If they choose correctly they gain a point. Then the game host reads out the first of the ten key research terms given to team B and team A have to make a choice from the three definitions presented by their opponents. Play continues until each team has presented all ten definitions. The team with the most points wins.

Optional Extension Activity

A useful extension activity for pupils wanting to develop their experimental techniques is to give pupils a practice research question and invite them to design an experimental method around it. Some ideas are given below but you probably have many of your own.

Design an experimental research method around one or more of the following research questions. Ensure that your design is ethical.

- Can computers increase skills in mental maths?
- To what extent is non-attendance in Year 6 pupils affected by attendance awards?
- How effective is peer mentoring in combatting bullying in schools?
- Can drama be an effective way to improve road safety awareness?

Key Reflection from Session 8

Experimental research is concerned with cause and effect, with the controlling and measuring of variables.

Suggested Further Reading

If you are interested in experimental methodology you might want to find out about 'quasi-experimental' techniques. There is a good section on this methodological approach in:

Robson, C. (2002) Real World Research (2nd edn), Oxford: Blackwell.

If you are interested in ethical dilemmas relating to quasi-experimental research with individuals who have learning difficulties, you might like to read:

Kellett, M. and Nind, M. (2001) Ethics in quasi-experimental research *on* people with severe learning disabilities: dilemmas and compromises, *British Journal of Learning Disabilities*, 29: 51–55.

PART III

Data Analysis

CHAPTER 9

Analysing Qualitative Data

Learning aims	Knowledge content	Skills	Interactive elements	Pupil follow-up work	Curriculum links
Begin to understand how to code and analyse qualitative data	Transcription First- and second-level coding Analysis of interview data	Organising, grouping and sifting large amounts of data Coding and categorising Memoing Theme abstracting	Group discussion Group coding and abstracting activity Expert Researcher card games	Coding and abstracting exercise	Citizenship PSHE RS Literacy

TEACHING CONTENT FOR SESSION 9

Timing: 120 minutes + 30 minutes follow-up work.

Introduction

Qualitative data refers to the kind of descriptive data commonly collected through interviews and observation. They are data in the form of words rather than numbers (quantitative data) and are often collected via audio or video recording and then transcribed. To transcribe something means to make an exact written copy of the conversations or audio observation notes. There are numerous methods of qualitative data analysis but I shall restrict the content of this chapter to those processes which can be most easily used by children. In essence, this requires an appreciation of three core aspects of qualitative data analysis: coding, memoing and abstracting.

Coding

Even short interviews or observation sessions can produce copious amounts of transcript data and finding ways of organising and managing these data can be challenging. A common technique used is *coding*. Coding is a way of helping to reduce the mass of data into manageable parts by grouping data into labelled categories so that themes and patterns can then be abstracted. Pupils will want to devise their own systems for coding, but the main points to remember are:

- Become very familiar with the data before attempting to code it, time given to any form of 'immersion process' is time well spent.

- Coding is meant to *reduce* the amount of data not increase it, so dissuade pupils from introducing too many categories.

- It is a good idea to have just a few main categories which can then be further divided into smaller subcategories if more are needed.

- Give each category a distinct definition and avoid overly similar categories where boundaries can become blurred.

- Decide on a code 'label' for each category, e.g. an abbreviation or a key word.

Memos

Alongside coding, qualitative researchers sometimes use a technique known as *memoing*. Memos are something we use in our everyday lives. They are short notes, written as reminders, and this is exactly the function of qualitative data 'memos'. They capture the researcher's ideas that occur during and after coding. These ideas can be anything the researcher feels to be relevant. The memos are the more intuitive side of analysis and contrast with the more systematic process of coding. But an important distinction is that while coding can be carried out in any reasonable time frame, memoing has to be done in the immediate moment, otherwise it ceases to be a memo and becomes more of a 'post-reflection conclusion'. During the dual process of coding and memoing, a qualitative researcher is constantly comparing what she or he sees in one coded data category with another. These comparisons feed directly into the abstraction process.

Abstraction

Abstracting themes is something most pupils begin to acquire at an early age through their reading comprehension activities and which they develop further in their later critiques of literature, history and fine art. It may be that some themes occur to the young researchers when they first 'immerse' themselves in the data. It is tempting to record these and consider the analysis complete. This would be to miss an important layer of the analysis process. Such observations are best recorded as memos in the first instance and returned to once a more detailed, coded analysis process has been accomplished.

From the first immersion in the transcript data, decide on four to six categories which cover the broad spectrum of the data. Then, systematically work through the transcript data allocating each interview quote or observation note to one of these categories. If you cannot decide where a particular datum fits, code it as 'Other' and return to it later. This is most easily done by writing a code identifier (e.g. an abbreviation or key word) alongside each datum. It is advisable to have the transcripts printed out with spacing between each quote for ease of management. Some pupils may prefer to use a colour-coded system.

The next stage is to group together all the data which relate to a particular category. I have found that a most effective way to do this is to encourage pupils to cut out each coded statement and gather them together in labelled piles or in labelled boxes. Then pupils analyse each 'pile' or 'box' in turn to see if they still agree with their initial coding and whether any additional categories or sub-codes should be introduced. Pupils then look at any data which has been put into the 'Other' pile and decide if they are now able to categorise these. Memoing can continue alongside these processes. These 'boxes' or 'piles' can also be reproduced in a grid format on a computer.

Once these organisational aspects are complete, pupils can begin more focused analysis of the data. This can include looking at the volume of quotes and/or observations in each pile – does the volume indicate any strong themes? Are there any patterns in the piles, e.g. are certain ages or genders migrating more towards one pile than another? Are there any surprises in the data? Are there any data which are especially difficult to code? The best way to gain an understanding of this analysis process is to experience it. The core activity for this chapter gives pupils an opportunity to try their hand at analysing some qualitative data. It uses real data collected by two 9-year old girls, Anna Carlini and Emma Barry, who carried out a research study exploring what life was like in the playground for girls who look much younger than their age (about three years younger). If you are interested in their study and how they put it together you can read their full account in Chapter 13.

BOX 9.1 KEY RESEARCH TERMS FOR SESSION 9

abstracting: a process of identifying common themes between and across sets of data.

coding (in qualitative research): attributing codes to data in order to reduce the data mass into manageable and thematic categories.

memoing: making immediate notes, throughout the initial stages of the analysis process, about aspects of the data, theory or research design that occur to the researcher.

Core Activity

You will need to use the transcripts in Photocopiable Resource 9 for this core activity. The young researchers used observation and interview to gather their data. The observations were undertaken over a period of two weeks during break time and consisted of observations made in real time and recorded into a Dictaphone. The transcript extracts are taken from break time observations of two 9-year-old girls, Kaz and Rose (their names have been changed for reasons of confidentiality). The activity can be done individually or in small groups.

Look through the transcript extracts and jot down any 'memos' that occur to you. Once you have read through the extracts and made some memos see if you can reduce the data by coding into categories. You will probably want to think up your own categories but here are a couple of suggestions to get you started:

Category 1 –Attention seeking –code AS

Category 2 –Being babied –code BB

Category 3 –Other –code O

As a group, decide on your categories, give them a code label (such as the 'AS' and 'BB' given above) then go through the extract meticulously and write your code labels alongside any observations that fit your categories. When you have done this, cut out the observation statements and organise them into category piles in the centre of your table. Look at the statements within each pile and across each pile. Can you make any connections? Can you draw any conclusions?

Guided comment

Here are some of the 'abstracted themes' that Anna and Emma came up with themselves and how they grouped the observation statements into categories.

Theme 1: Being treated like a cuddly doll

- Her friends kept picking her up.
- Her friends kept swinging and twirling Kaz around (holding Kaz around her middle).
- Kaz was being hugged quite a lot (no one else in the group was being hugged).
- Rose got picked up quite a lot.
- Rose got twirled round a lot.
- Friends were playing at trying to 'stretch' Rose.

Theme 2: Trying hard to get attention

- Kaz kept hanging onto people in her group.
- Kaz kept gripping on to friends' hands and arms.
- Kaz often shouted loudly and if nobody took any notice she shouted louder and louder. She was shouting the loudest in the group.
- Rose kept clinging on to people.
- Rose tried to pull people away to get their attention.
- Rose kept hanging onto people's arms and pulling them.
- Rose was yelling a lot louder than anyone else in the group.

Theme 3: Actions linked to small size

- Kaz was often crouching down low to the ground.
- Kaz was ducking.
- Kaz was hanging on to friends from behind (almost hiding behind them).
- If Kaz got 'caught' in the tag game she yelled more often (and more loudly) than the others to get free and usually friends came straight away to get her free –more quickly than any of the others.
- When playing tag, Rose did not get chased as much as the others.

- If Rose tried to 'take charge' most ignored her.
- If another person in the group started talking when Rose was talking the others ignored Rose and started to listen to the new person.
- Rose kept running off and nobody bothered about her and I think nobody noticed that she had run off –this might have been because she was so much smaller.
- Rose dept 'ducking' a lot.

Differentiating the core activity

Advanced level

The qualitative data analysis technique described in this chapter is a simplified version of an approach known as Grounded Theory (Glaser and Strauss, 1967; Strauss and Corbin, 1997) where three 'layers' of coding are sequentially intro-duced. The first is a general level of coding, *open coding*, when the researcher 'breaks open' the data and looks for categories to create at a general level. The second layer of coding is *axial coding*, where the categories from the first cod-ing sift are re-examined to see what possible connections there are between the categories and this frequently leads to a re-categorisation of the data at a more 'interconnected' level. The third stage of coding is *selective coding*, where spe-cific themes or 'concepts' are extracted. It is these concepts which lead to the generation of new theory. Pupils who are interested in the grounded theory approach can find out more in the suggested further reading at the end of the chapter. They might also like to try analysing the interview transcripts from Photocopiable Resource 6 using the principles of grounded theory.

Simpler level

Pupils could code and analyse the extracts with just the two suggested cate-gories of 'being babied' (BB) and 'attention seeking' (AS) using differently coloured highlighter pens.

Follow-up Work

Pupils can practise their qualitative data analysis skills on other transcript data. Sometimes original transcript data are included as an appendix at the end of a research study. This is done where researchers want to make their analysis claims transparent and accountable and is generally always done in research degree theses. Teachers may have data of their own or know a colleague who has suitable transcript material. Alternatively, pupils can work from one of the photocopiable interview transcripts provided in Photocopiable Resource 6.

Expert Researcher Card Games

Make cards for the three new key research terms and definitions given in Box 9.1.

Game 9: Poached pairs

This game can be played with two, three or four players, but is most fun when played with four. Shuffle the cards and deal four cards to each player which they keep hidden in their hand. An additional four cards are dealt to each player but these are turned face up in front of the players and must remain on view to all players for the duration of the game unless they are legitimately 'poached' by one of the players. The remaining cards are placed in a pile face down in the centre of the table.

Players keep a careful watch on the four cards hidden in their hand as well as their face-up cards and the face-up cards of their opponents. Strictly in turn, each player has an opportunity to make a matching pair. This must be done by using *one card from the hidden hand* and one from any of the face-up cards, whether this is the player's own or an opponent's. Let us imagine Karina begins. If she wants to 'poach' a card from an opponent she has to replace the poached card with one from her hidden hand. Similarly if she wants to match a pair using her own face-up card she has to replace this from one in her own hand. Players get to keep any matched pairs they make. Karina's turn is completed by picking up a single card from the central pile and adding it to her hidden hand. *Only one matched pair is allowed per turn even if players can make more than one pair*. If Karina cannot make a pair then she simply picks up a card from the central pile to add to her hidden hand. Play then passes to the next person who has an opportunity to similarly try and match up a pair. Play continues until all the pairs are matched or until a stalemate is reached. The winner is the player with the most matched pairs.

Key Reflection from Session 9

Do not rush qualitative data analysis. Allow time to 'immerse' yourself in the data before beginning the process of coding and abstracting.

Suggested Further Reading

Mason, J. (2002) *Qualitative Researching* (2nd edn), London: Sage.

CHAPTER 10

Analysing Quantitative Data

Learning aims	Knowledge content	Skills	Interactive elements	Pupil follow-up work	Curriculum links
Begin to understand some of the approaches to quantitative analysis and how this differs from qualitative analysis	Find ways to compare sets of data in a valid way	Expression of data in tabular form	Group discussion	Quantitative data analysis exercise	Maths
	Statistical significance	Importance of sample size	Quantitative data analysis activity		Science
Develop strategies for handling large quantities of raw data		Use of percentages	Expert Researcher card games		Geography
		Graphical representation of data			Citizenship

TEACHING CONTENT FOR SESSION 10

Timing: 120 minutes + 30 minutes follow-up work.

Introduction

In the last chapter we looked at some techniques for coding and analysing qualitative data. These were approaches which can be used with descriptive data, i.e. data in the form of words. Researchers also collect data in the form of numbers –quantitative data –so we need to have some basic understanding of how we might go about analysing numerical data. Some descriptive data can also be attributed a numerical score in order to facilitate quantitative analysis. The advantage of quantitative analysis is that statistical operations can be used to measure and analyse effects. This can be done with extremely large sets of data. One of the studies (Pickett, 2004) in *The Reality of Research with Children and Young People* (see suggested further reading, Chapter 2) analysed the responses from a survey of 50,000 young people aged 11 to 15 years across 12 countries about their attitudes to risky health behaviour. Where large amounts of data are concerned computer software is generally used to help the researcher carry out different kinds of statistical analysis.

Quantitative Observational Data

In quantitative research observation data are represented numerically rather than descriptively. This is done by assigning a code to a particular behaviour and then measuring how many times this behaviour occurs in a given situation or in a given time (more information on coding can be found in Chapter 5). Using the earlier mixed gender football example, let us consider that a researcher might be interested in whether boys are more likely to pass the ball to boys than to girls in schools where mixed gender football is not normally played. Supposing the researcher set up and video-taped ten mixed gender football matches in each of two primary schools, one school where mixed gender football was played regularly and actively encouraged by teachers (e.g. membership of a mixed football league), and one school where mixed gender football was played only occasionally (e.g. fun events). From the video data, the researcher recorded how many times boys passed the ball to boys and how many times boys passed the ball to girls in a set time (e.g. 20 minutes). If teams, in each school consisted of five girls and five boys plus a goalkeeper of either gender then, providing the researcher discounted any passes made by the goalkeeper, the design would be a fair one. We could call the school that rarely played mixed gender football school A and the other one school B. Some data to illustrate this are presented in Tables 10.1 and 10.2.

Because of the different numbers of passes in the games a researcher would first need to convert the data into percentages so that each game was being analysed on the same basis, as shown in Table 10.3.

A word of caution about percentages. In the example given in Table 10.3 the expression of the data as percentages is helpful and appropriate because the comparison of passes between the genders is based on similar numbers of boys and girls, i.e. between similar numbers in different data sets. However, there are occasions when representing data as percentages can be misleading. Consider an example where a researcher is interested in gender differences in attitudes to school uniform. He designs a questionnaire and gives this to members of his year group. Results from the returned questionnaire make up two sets of data, one for each gender. The researcher converts the figures from

Table 10.1 Results for school A

Football match	Passes by boys to boys	Passes by boys to girls	Total number of passes
1	31	9	40
2	26	20	46
3	17	16	33
4	38	5	43
5	19	17	36
6	32	10	42
7	43	29	72
8	27	11	38
9	25	16	41
10	21	12	33

Table 10.2 Results for school B

Football match	Passes by boys to boys	Passes by boys to girls	Total number of passes
1	49	5	54
2	37	3	40
3	39	4	43
4	60	8	68
5	51	8	59
6	42	6	48
7	43	9	52
8	48	9	57
9	66	10	76
10	42	7	49

these two data sets into percentages for ease of comparison. He concludes that 75 per cent of girls dislike wearing school uniform compared with 50 per cent of boys. On the surface this seems to be a straightforward process. But the researcher fails to acknowledge the number of pupils in the year group and the number of returned questionnaires by each gender. In actual fact there were 50 girls and 50 boys in the year group, 48 boys returned his questionnaire but only four girls. Therefore his 75 per cent claim relates to three girls out of a possible 50 compared to 48 boys out of a possible 50, resulting in a rather unsound conclusion. This is not to say that percentages can only be used when data sets have equal numbers. One of the great advantages of percentages is that they can help to illuminate comparisons between non-equal sets of data

Table 10.3 Number of passes expressed as percentages

Football match	School A				School B			
	Passes by boys to boys	Passes by boys to girl	Total number of passes	% passes boys to girls*	Passes by boys to boys	Passes by boys to girls	Total number of passes	% passes boys to girls*
1	31	9	40	23	49	5	54	9
2	26	20	46	44	37	3	40	8
3	17	16	33	49	39	4	43	9
4	38	5	43	12	60	8	68	12
5	19	17	36	47	51	8	59	14
6	32	10	42	24	42	6	48	13
7	43	29	72	40	43	9	52	17
8	27	11	38	30	48	9	57	16
9	25	16	41	39	66	10	76	13
10	21	12	33	36	42	7	49	14
Totals	279	145	424	34**	477	69	546	13**

* Rounded to the nearest whole per cent. **average % from the 10 matches

but *all* the facts must be declared so that the process is transparent and can be scrutinised. Pupils will probably have come across the use of '*n* = .'. in their reading of some of the recommended research papers. This is the conventional way of declaring the total number in a data set. Staying with the school uniform example, the researcher should have presented his findings as:

Question	Percentage of girls responding yes $n = 4$	Percentage of boys responding yes $n = 48$
Do you dislike wearing school uniform?	75%	50%

Core Activity

This core activity involves some active quantitative data analysis and can be found in a convenient format in Photocopiable Resource 10. Pupils should scrutinise the data provided in Table 10.3 and write about or discuss what they can deduce from the data. Encourage them to think about whether:

- a valid comparison is being made across the two sets of data
- what conclusions can be drawn?

These data only relate to two schools. Is this enough to be able to make any generalisations about mixed gender football? To generalise means to take a finding from one situation and apply it in a wider context – e.g. could a researcher take the findings from these two schools and apply them to all schools in the UK? This brings us back to considerations of sample size again and also to something else that is important in the analysis of some quantitative data, statistical significance. Teaching of statistical significance may only be appropriate for older or highly able younger pupils and therefore, rather than differentiate the core activity for these groups of pupils, I have included additional teaching material in the section on statistical significance.

Analysing Comparative Data

A common methodological approach in quantitative research uses a comparative group design. Here, sets of data are collected in order to compare them for differences or similarities. Supposing a researcher wants to investigate whether there is a link between eye colour and the wearing of spectacles in 13-year-olds. The researcher might hypothesise that more blue-eyed 13-year-olds wear glasses than brown-eyed 13-year-olds. His or her research question might be: *Do more blue-eyed 13-year-olds wear spectacles than brown-eyed 13-year-olds?*

The methodological design is relatively simple and straightforward. The researcher needs to access sample populations of blue-eyed 13-year-olds and brown-eyed 13-year-olds and find out from each of them whether they wear spectacles or not. However care still has to be taken. What other factors might the researcher have to consider?

- Sample size –this would need to be large enough to be seen to be representative of general population trends.

- Extraneous variables –what other conditions might account for the wearing of spectacles other than eye colour? For example, gender might be a possible variable here. The researcher could either prepare a subset of data based on gender, or control for this variable by restricting the population samples to a single gender, e.g. *Do more blue-eyed 13-year-old girls wear spectacles than brown-eyed 13-year-old girls?*

Let us imagine that the researcher collects data from a random sample of 150 blue-eyed 13-year-old girls and 150 brown-eyed 13-year-old girls in a large comprehensive school and that these are the results.

Blue-eyed with spectacles		Blue-eyed without spectacles		Brown-eyed with spectacles		Brown-eyed without spectacles	
$n = 150$				$n = 150$			
Number	Percentage	Number	Percentage	Number	Percentage	Number	Percentage
22	14.7	128	85.3	11	7.3	139	92.7

According to these results, twice as many blue-eyed girls wear glasses compared to brown-eyed girls. This could be a very interesting finding, but how far can this be generalised to the whole population of 13-year-old blue-eyed and brown-eyed girls? Clearly, the quoted sample size is very small. The closer the sample size is to the full population size, the more confident a researcher can be about generalisation. If data has been collected from the entire UK population of blue-eyed and brown-eyed 13-year-olds then the researcher could be entirely confident of the findings. However, this would be an unusually large sample size and it is more common for researchers to work from proportionately smaller samples –although a sample size of six is not going to be at all convincing in this instance. To avoid a somewhat messy and arbitrary system of generalisation, researchers have devised a procedure to determine this based around the mathematical laws of probability. It is a procedure called *statistical significance*.

Statistical Significance

This section may not be suitable for younger or less able pupils. Statistical significance relates to whether the differences showing in the data are bigger or smaller than the differences which might be expected to have happened by chance. In other words, statistical significance is concerned with how likely it is that the researcher got it wrong and the results are merely due to chance rather than the researcher's attributable cause (i.e. that blue eyes are more prone to short sight than brown eyes). How do we work out the likelihood of this? The good news is that these calculations are done for us in tables of statistical inference which appear in most statistics books and in other sources such as some commonly available computer software. Basically, how it works is that a statistic from the research data (e.g. the statistic that twice as many blue-eyed girls wear glasses as brown-eyed girls) is compared through distributions in the statistical inference tables to find out the mathematical likelihood of this happening by chance. Generally speaking, the probability of something happening by chance is taken as being no greater than five in a hundred times ($p = 0.05$). Once the p values for your data are worked out (from statistical inference tables) these can be compared with the $p = 0.05$ value to check for statistical significance. If your p values are smaller than this ($p<0.05$) then the data are accepted as statistically significant. For example if the p value was 0.02 then this would be statistically significant. The smaller the p value, the more statistically significant your data can be shown to be, (e.g. $p = 0.001$ is highly statistically significant) and the greater the generalisability of the findings.

There is considerable controversy surrounding statistical significance testing. One of the major problems is that statistical significance is not related to the size or importance of the actual effect that is being measured, it only relates to the size of the probability that the results could have happened by chance. Because of this, some researchers prefer to rely on descriptive statistics where the focus is more on the size of the effect. When pupils undertake their own research they will need to decide on what methods of analysis are most suited to their research question and their sample size. Even if they do use statistical significance testing, it is advisable not to rely on this as their only form of analysis.

Advanced level activity

How would you go about analysing the raw data in Table 10.4? What can you deduce from the data? What conclusions (if any) can you draw? Do you need to consider levels of statistical significance?

BOX 10.1 KEY RESEARCH TERMS FOR SESSION 10

statistical significance: is a measure of whether the differences of the effect showing in the data are bigger or smaller than the differences which might be expected to have happened by chance.

Follow-up Work

An additional set of quantitative data is provided in Photocopiable Resource 10a for pupils wanting to do some follow-up work. Alternative sets of data can be found in the results sections of some research studies and in archive databases located on the Internet. The data on the number of passes in the mixed gender football example in Tables 10.1 and 10.2 could also be analysed for statistical significance testing.

Table 10.4 Data about bullying in Flowerbed Comprehensive School

Year group	Number of girls in year group	Number of boys in year group	Number of girls who have been bullied		Number of boys who have been bullied	
			By own age pupils	By older pupils	By own age pupils	By older pupils
Y7	80	72	4	14	14	17
Y8	70	79	8	11	10	11
Y9	52	96	7	7	8	12
Y10	71	77	13	4	5	2
Y11	78	64	16	2	2	0

Expert Researcher Card Games

Make cards for the new key research term and its definition. Game 10 requires the preparation of a set of domino cards. Using the Collated Glossary Sheet from Photocopiable Resource 12 prepare a set of cards where one half of the card carries a key research term and the second half of the divided card carries a definition but this must not be a matching one. Here is an example:

participant observation	a group interview with a focused theme where interpersonal dynamics and the interaction of participants to one another's comments forms an important element in the data.

Game 10: Domino square

Shuffle the domino cards and then spread them out face up on a large table. Individually, in pairs or small groups, pupils attempt to match up one end of a domino card with its correct key term or definition and continue with this process until they have matched all the cards and joined them up into a rectangle.

Key Reflection from Session 10

Quantitative research is concerned with the *measurement* of effects and it is important that the means used for measuring such effects can be shown to be reliable and valid.

Suggested Further Reading

Chapter 13, Analysis of quantitative data, in Robson, C. (2002) *Real World Research*, (2nd edn), Oxford: Blackwell.

Dissemination

CHAPTER 11

Producing a Research Report

Learning aims	Knowledge content	Skills	Interactive elements	Pupil follow-up work	Curriculum links
To produce a clear, comprehensive account of a research study To adapt the mode of dissemination for different audiences	Conventions of research writing	Clarity of expression Organisational skills Persuasive argument Redrafting skills	Peer review Expert Researcher card games	Research report	Literacy

TEACHING CONTENT FOR SESSION 11

Timing: 90 minutes + sufficient time to complete a research report.

Introduction

For pupils who have undertaken a research study which they have chosen, designed and carried out themselves, the dissemination process becomes particularly important because it enhances their sense of ownership and has a positive effect on confidence and self-esteem. Reporting can be done at several levels: a presentation to the pupil research group; a special assembly; a presentation to governing bodies or presentations on larger platforms such as conference venues. A formal report of the study (this can be in many forms other than a written report) helps package pupils' projects in a format which is easily adapted for different audiences such as dissemination on websites, the media and publishing outlets. Pupils from Year 6 upwards should be familiar with software such as PowerPoint and will enjoy the challenge of putting together an oral presentation. There is more on PowerPoint presentations in Chapter 12. Spurred on by their research activity some pupils I have worked with have presented at high-profile conferences (Research in Practice, Westminster Institute of Education, 16 June 2003; Spotlight on Learning, National Union of Teachers, 26 May 2004; Powerful Voices, Ealing Borough, 25 June 2004), and disseminated in the media *Times Educational Supplement*, 7 November 2003; BBC Radio 4, 25 November 2003; the *Guardian*, 23 March 2004 and the *Independent*, 6 July 2004) and some even presented at a Cabinet Office forum (3 June 2004).

The Written Report

A research report is essentially telling a story. It tells the story of how researchers came to do their research (the introduction), how they went about it (the methodology), what happened (the results), what the findings tell us (the discussion) and what we can all learn from this (the conclusions). As with any good story it needs to have lots of detail. While the research is very familiar to the author, a reader probably knows little or nothing about it, so it is important that a level of detail is included which enables a reader to put the pieces together. It is easy to forget to describe things that are very obvious, e.g. how many people participated in the research or the location/context of the research or the time frames. It is essential that the names of participants and establishments are changed to enable confidentiality to be maintained.

Set out in Photocopiable Resource 11a is a writing frame designed to help pupils in the drafting stage of their written report. It is divided into boxed sections according to the five main research reporting conventions or 'story themes' as they were identified above. Each box has a few prompts about the sorts of things to include in each section of the report and suggestions of how much pupils might write. These amounts are based on average reports that other children have produced and are only a guide –e.g. one report ran to 17 pages whereas another was only two pages.

Developing Pupils' Research Report Writing Skills

As we discovered in Chapter 2, critical reading of other people's research is a skill which can be developed and good report writing is also a skill which improves with guidance and practice. The key development areas to focus on for research report writing are organisation, structure, clarity and style. The remainder of this chapter is given over to suggested activities for developing these skills in pupils.

Organisation and structure

There are some basic pointers to good research writing whether this is at school pupil or PhD student level. Organisation and structure are the cornerstones. The report writing frame in Photocopiable Resource 11a provides a starting point for the basic structure. Encourage pupils to put plenty of 'signposts' in their reports indicating what they intend to tell the reader and in what part of the report they will do this. Separate the main parts of the report into sections and organise these with headings and subheadings. Different font sizes and the use of italic and other styles can help with the general organisation and navigation although overuse makes the presentation too fussy and complex. Keep it clear and simple. There should always be a good reason for a font change, e.g. for emphasis or effect. Bullet points are a useful way of summarising and organising information. Tables and graphs are good ways to display data rather than lengthy word descriptions. Writing is always enhanced by good linkage between sentences and between paragraphs so that the flow is organised and logical.

Clarity and style

Pupils' reports may well be read by a wide audience ranging from their peers to headteachers, community practitioners, professors and politicians. Most are unlikely to be familiar with their topic, so pupils will need to consider whether to provide explanations as well as descriptions. Avoid long, rambling sentences and aim to cover only one point in a single sentence. Clarity is lost when the writing 'darts around' so keep points closely related to, and following on from, one another. If pupils need to criticise anyone else's research in the introduction to their report or disagree with others' conclusions, this should be done in a respectful way. However, it is also important that pupils' reports speak with the voices of young people since the young person perspective is an important part of the original contribution to knowledge. Therefore, it is quite acceptable –and to be encouraged –that in the introduction and discussion sections of the report, pupils allow their own voice and style to come through. By contrast, the methodology and findings sections should have a neutral, objective style because they are simply transferring information about the study rather than discussing any inferences or implications.

Alternatives to the Written Report

In my experience the research reporting phase is the least favourite part of a research project for pupils and some of them can become disheartened at this stage. The process of engaging in research is the most important learning tool rather than the act of writing itself and it may be that pupils prefer to make an audio tape instead. If an adult helps by transcribing this for pupils then they can work on it in the same way as they would on any first writing draft. Some pupils may also need help to translate raw data into tables and graphs so that they can more easily analyse their data.

An increasingly popular reporting genre is video documentary and this format is particularly attractive to pupils who do not have strong literacy skills or are reluctant writers. Video can be a very effective way of presenting all or part of a research project, in the form of a 'mini-documentary'. Clips of video data can be included as short illustrative sequences (provided they have all the appropriate consents from participants). Such clips are easily edited using Mac software 'imovie' or similar digital video software packages. Pupils can record and edit short video sequences about different stages of their research, including 'talking to camera', or adding voice-over commentary to explain what they did and why.

Once all the raw material for the video has been recorded this is imported into a computer where editing can begin. When making a video about their research project, pupils require many of the skills used by documentary film-makers. Initially, pupils should create a 'first assembly' with all the video clips made into a rough 'storyboard' sequence. These can then be further edited and polished to include professional effects such as fade-ins, transitions, sound effects, voice-over commentary, music and titles.

Editing is great fun but takes a lot of time. Pupils could easily spend several weeks editing a five minute presentation. So the best advice is not to be too ambitious. If pupils get too carried away with all the 'special effects' the content and message of their research might become buried in all the extravaganza. A simple, short, well-planned video documentary can be an extremely effective way to disseminate pupils' research.

Core Activity

You will need Photocopiable Resource 11b for this activity. It is an example of a first draft research report which has been put together in a rather muddled fashion. It is an interesting research study with some important findings but in its present form is not easy for readers to follow. Reorganise and redraft the text so that it has a clearer structure. Delete any text you regard as irrelevant. Is there anything missing from the report?

Optional Extension Activity

Some pupils you work with may want to aim to get their work published in a journal or the media and may feel able to undertake a simple literature review of the topic they are covering. This involves reading around the topic and finding out what other research has been done in the same field. Rather than just summarising other people's arguments, a good literature review compares and contrasts these views, pointing out where there have been differences of opinion and who has influenced what, where and when. Encourage pupils to reflect on what surprises them, on some of the points they would like to learn more about and where there are any gaps in the research.

Pupils should resist the temptation to simply produce a 'shopping list' of what has been written about their topic. The prompt questions below might help to develop their review skills.

- What are the origins and definitions of this topic?
- How does this relate to my research question(s)?
- What are the major issues and debates?
- What are the main questions and ideas that have been researched to date?
- How has the literature increased knowledge and understanding of the topic?
- What are the main sources that support my line of argument?
- What are the main sources that question my line of argument?
- Are there any areas that have not been previously explored in the literature?
- What is my personal stance/position/opinion?

Publication Opportunities

Research undertaken by children makes an original contribution to knowledge about childhood, children's lives and children's learning. Some studies may be of interest, therefore, to editors of academic journals, education magazines and the media. Submissions to referred journals are generally reviewed 'blind' in a process where the reviewers do not know the identity of the author(s). It would be helpful, therefore, if there were some indication early on, perhaps in the abstract or introduction that the author(s) are young researchers as opposed to adult researchers so that the study can be judged in that context. Journals all differ in the length of article required. Some can be as short as 1,500 words, others 6,000 words and many are looking for articles of 3,000-4,000 words. This is a daunting prospect for the average pupil. Able 10-year-olds can generally produce a report of 1,500 words without too much difficulty. To support pupils seeking external publishing opportunities it is best to study a journal over a period of time to get a feel for the kind of research it features and its style. If you are setting up a Research Club in your school or a long-term timetabled commitment to research activity, it might be worth subscribing to a journal such as *Children & Society* or *Childhood*. A lot of encouragement and support will be required for pupils who want to do an extended piece of work, especially as this is likely to require a review of existing literature. Sometimes it is a good idea for two or three pupils to get together to combine their projects in one article which might then be of interest to a journal editor. Alternatively, teachers and practitioners themselves might like to co-author a paper with pupils. In these circumstances issues around ownership need to be handled sensitively. The Children's Research Centre at the Open University is always interested in research undertaken by children and young people and will actively consider submissions for publication on its website. You can contact them at http://childrens-research-centre.open.ac.uk. Also, some children's charities such as Save the Children, the Children's Society and Carnegie Youth Trust may be interested in children's work for their websites.

Expert Researcher Card Games

You will need to use the sets of domino cards from Chapter 10. In this more traditional game of dominoes, pupils play in competition with one another rather than in collaboration as they did for the domino square game. The game works best with three players.

Game 11: Dominoes

Shuffle the domino cards and deal out five to each player and put the remaining domino cards in a pile face down on the table. The top card is turned over and placed face up in the centre of the table. In turn, players try to find a domino from their hand which matches with one or other half of the face-up domino card (either the key term or the definition). If they have a matching card they place it end to end with its pair, producing a new term or definition which needs to be matched. If players cannot find a match they must take a card from the pile and add it to their hand. The winner is the first to discard all the domino cards in her or his hand.

Key Reflection from Session 11

A research report is essentially telling a story. It tells the story of how you came to do your research, how you went about it, what happened and what we can all learn from what you found out.

Suggested Further Reading

Chapter 8, Writing up, in Blaxter, L., Hughes, C. and Tight, M. (2001) *How to Research*, (2nd edn), Buckingham: Open University Press.

CHAPTER 12

Presentation Skills

Learning aims	Knowledge content	Skills	Interactive elements	Pupil follow-up work	Curriculum links
To develop confident and effective presentation skills	Effective presentation	Planning and organisation Time keeping Voice projection PowerPoint skills	Mock presentations Expert Researcher card games	PowerPoint slide show	IT Literacy PSHE Citizenship

TEACHING CONTENT FOR SESSION 12

Timing: 90 minutes plus time to prepare a PowerPoint presentation.

PowerPoint Presentations

A five- or ten-minute oral presentation by each young researcher is a good end goal to have and is an incentive for pupils who find the 'writing up' stage of their research heavy going. Most pupils should be familiar with PowerPoint from Year 6 upwards and will enjoy creating their own 'slide show'. The bank of design templates in the software package provides plenty of scope and pupils will delight in adding animation and importing picture illustrations. If they have collected photographic or video data, samples of these can be incorporated into their PowerPoint presentation, as can graphs and tables. Here are a few tips for pupils for effective PowerPoint presentations.

- Make the slides attractive but not too 'busy'.
- Use a font size of at least 16.
- Animation is fun but too much can detract from the mes-

sage you are trying to get across in the presentation.

- Do not prepare too many slides –aim to talk for approximately one minute per slide.

- Prepare a full script of what you want to say for each slide and then crystallise this into a few key points with short, written prompts (these short, written prompts can be put onto the 'three-to-a-page handouts' which give space alongside each slide for notes. These are available via the Print menu on the PowerPoint software package).

- Make a conscious effort to speak more slowly than conversational speech (nerves tend to cause us to speed up).

- If presenting without a microphone, practise projecting your voice. Aim to speak at three times your normal conversational level, this is to enable your voice to penetrate to the back of a large room and to enable your voice to rise above the noise of projection equipment. Aim to 'throw' your voice to the back of the room rather than at the front two rows.

- Practise speaking into two types of microphone: a fixed-stand microphone and a lapel-style microphone. These require different techniques. The fixed microphone requires you to stand relatively still and keep the distance between the mouth and the microphone as constant as possible to produce an even tone without words fading in and out with each head or body movement. A lapel-style microphone is easier to use as it follows you rather than the other way round but you still need to practise getting the speaking level right for the size of room. Always remember to switch a lapel-style microphone off when you are not presenting, unless you want all your private conversations to be broadcasted!

Presentation Opportunities

There is currently a lot of interest in child-led research and there may well be external presentation opportunities for pupils you are working with. If you are located near to a university it would be worth making contact with the Education and/or Childhood departments to see if there are any seminars/conferences where child researchers would be welcome. Some children's charities and community groups also welcome young researchers onto their platforms.

Consider hosting a 'Pupils as Researchers Conference' event at your own school. Embrace the concept of child researchers contributing to school improvement and to continuing professional development for staff. This might involve pupils who have researched topics such as bullying or pupil behaviour or explored attitudes to learning and curriculum issues doing presentations to governing bodies, school councils or staff meetings.

Core Activity and Follow-up Work

Both the core activity and follow-up sessions are given over to time for pupils to explore and experiment with PowerPoint design, aiming to produce a short PowerPoint presentation of five to ten minutes about their research which they present to their peers.

Expert Researcher Card Games

This is a non-competitive game that can be played singly or in pairs. Players will need to use the domino cards for this game.

Game 12: Match or bust

Shuffle all the domino cards and deal out *four* domino cards in a row from left to right. The first three are placed face down and the fourth is left face up. Then start a new row and deal *three* domino cards from left to right –partially, but not completely covering, the first row of cards so that they peep out from underneath –the first two are placed face down and the third is left face up. Start a third row and deal *two* cards in the same way with the first one placed face down and the second face up. Finish with a fourth row where a single domino card is placed face up. The remaining cards are kept together in a pile on the table. Play begins by turning the top card over from the pile and placing it in the centre of the table. If a match can be found for either side of this domino starter card from any of the face up cards this is placed end to end with the starter card. When any face up card is used then the next card above it in the column is turned over to reveal it. If this happens to be the column where there is only one face-up card and its removal leaves an empty column the player can choose one of two actions: (1) move any face-up card into the empty space and then turn over the face-down card which has now reached the bottom of its column (at any one time all bottom cards in each column should be face up); (2) deal a card from the top of the pile face up into the empty space. Play continues until no more matches and card shifting can be done. Then two cards are peeled off from the top of the pack to the bottom without being seen but then the third card is turned over to reveal it. If it matches with either end of the domino train it can be added to the train; if not it goes to the bottom of the pile. Once again, two cards are peeled off from the top of the pack to the bottom unseen and the third card is turned over. If it matches with either end of the domino train it can be added; if not it goes to the bottom of the pile as before. Continue in this way, watching carefully to see if any addition to the domino train results in one of the face up cards being able to be played, thus prompting actions (1) or (2) above and uncovering another of the concealed cards. The idea of the game is to be able to uncover all the concealed cards so that between those and the cards in the pile the train will be able to be completed. As with any patience-like game this will not always be possible and if players reach a stalemate position they are 'bust'. It is imperative that no cards are missing from the domino pack and a careful check should be carried out before starting the game to avoid unnecessary frustration.

Key Reflection from Session 12

Pupil researchers can make a valuable contribution to school development and improvement.

Suggested Further Reading

http://childrens-research-centre.open.ac.uk.

Children as Active Researchers

This chapter contains three studies by child researchers aged between 10 and 12 years of age. The reports are diverse in topic, illustrate different methods and vary in length and style. A sense of ownership is evident in all of them and, importantly, a unique young person perspective comes through strongly. They constitute an original contribution to knowledge and demonstrate what can be achieved by children actively researching issues that interest or concern them. The first report was undertaken by a Year 7 pupil, the second by two Year 6 pupils and the third report by two Year 5 pupils.

How Does Death Affect Children?

(by Paul O'Brien, Year 7)

Introduction

I was interested in how children are affected by death and how it might change their behaviour. This could be the death of a pet or a relative –and if it was a relative, how it might be different if it was a close relative or a distant relative. I was interested in this subject because I wanted to see if it may play a part in the way that some people I know behave. I wanted to find out what children thought about their own behaviour and if they thought it changed them when someone they cared about died. I also wanted to know what they thought death was.

I looked for what I could find about what other people say about death and children of my age. I found a study by Robin F Goodman PhD on the NYU Child Study Centre website. In it he says that 'By age 9 or 10 children have acquired a mature understanding of death. They know that: (1) it is a permanent state; (2) it cannot be reversed; (3) once you have died your body is no longer able to function; (4) it will happen to everyone at some time; (5) it will happen to them.'

My research question was 'How are children affected by death and how does it change them, and change their behaviour?'

Methodology

I wanted to find out the views of children my age but I realised death is a difficult subject. So I decided the most ethical way of finding out the information I needed was to ask permission to talk to the children about it. I designed a short questionnaire which asked them:

- Have you ever had a pet die? Please tick all that apply. (cat, dog, hamster, mouse, rabbit, other pet)
- Have you ever had a death in your family? Tick all that apply.

  (mum, dad, sister, brother, grandma, granddad, uncle, aunt, other relative)
- Would you be willing to talk to me about it?

I handed this out to 160 children of ages 9, 10, 11 and 12 at my school. They filled it out in class and I collected the results in on the same day. I took the results home and picked out eight students to interview. In choosing the eight I looked for a variety of different types of bereavement. I also tried to get people from a variety of different countries and religions, and to get girls as well as boys. Because my interest in this topic came from my own experience I decided to focus on people from my own age group so all my interviewees were from Year 7. Also as death is a difficult subject to talk about I felt more comfortable talking to people I already knew well because I am in Year 7.

I interviewed these students three weeks after the survey as it took time to look through their forms. I did all the interviews on the same day during school time. I was able to use the ICT suite to make it private so nobody could listen in. Each interview lasted about 15 minutes. There was a range of questions about different emotions and different stages of the bereavement. I was trying to make the students as comfortable as possible, as I knew it was an upsetting subject for them to talk about, I gave them a choice of taping the interview using a Dictaphone or for them to write the answers down on an interview sheet.

The findings

Figure 13.1 shows the results of the exploratory questionnaire in which 145 children ranging from age 9-12 indicated whether they had experienced the death of a family member, or a pet, or both, or none. All but one of the children had experienced at least one death.

I organised the answers from the interviews into groups and then put these together into a table so I could compare them more easily. Now I will discuss the answers and themes of each question in turn. Every one of my interviewees had lost one or more relatives. Only two of them had lost pets. Most of the relatives or pets had died in the last 1-5 years.

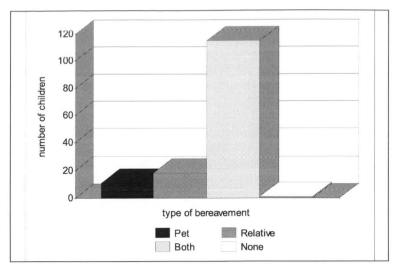

Figure 13.1   Responses to question about whether children aged 9–12 had experienced death
(*n*=145)

Q1   Can you describe to me how it felt when you found out your relative/pet had died?

Everyone spoke about their sadness. For those who lost pets it seemed to be just as hard and upsetting as for someone who had lost a relative like a grandparent. One person I interviewed said as well as sadness they felt regret as they had not seen the relative who died for two months.

Q2   How would you say you dealt with the death overall?

There was a mixed reaction here as half my interviewees thought they had handled the death very well. But the other half told me about the difficulties they had had. One girl said it took her a month to recover from her experience of death. One boy told me he cried for a week after the death. Another boy said the hardest part was accepting his grandparent was dead. 'The hardest part was just to get round that granddad was dead. I used to do nearly everything with him.'

Q3   Who supported you most through the death?

All but one person I interviewed said it was their family who helped them most, and for most of them their mum and dad were the biggest factor in getting them through the death. In two cases people found it helpful that their families did not talk about it much because they knew it would upset them. Although I asked whether they'd had help from friends or teachers, no-one had gone to those people for support.

Q4   How did they support you?

Two people said they were taken on holiday to take their minds off the death. Another person said what helped her was 'I was told that he was always going to be watching and that he will always love you.' One girl said she was helped by knowing her family understood her sadness because they felt the same way.

Q5   What was the hardest part of dealing with the death?

Two people said the hardest part was before the death actually happened but they knew it was going to. Two others said it was the shock of the death that was the hardest. One boy found the most difficult thing to deal with was when others mentioned the death.

Q6   Did anything confuse you about the death?

Those who answered this said that it was understanding why their relative had to die that was the most confusing. One girl said: 'The most confusing thing was that he was dying cos he was always in a fit state and he wasn't ready to go.' The other thing that someone found confusing was that their relative was not going to be there anymore.

Q7   Do you feel that this death has changed you in any way?

Five of the eight interviewees said that it had changed the way they feel about life. Two of them said they now appreciate life a lot more. 'Live each day to the full,' one told me. Another one said: 'You should always be nice to mum and dad because they will not be there for ever.' Two people said it affected their personality and the way they behaved for a while. One boy explained that he knew now he could not stay with one person for a lifetime. 'I have to find other people.'

Q8   Has experiencing death taught you anything about life?

People again talked about feeling that you should live life to the full and you shouldn't take things or people for granted. Two of the interviewees told me it had taught them that death comes to everybody. One said: 'It taught me that once you're born you have to die sometime, young or old.'

Q9   Do you still get emotional or have you recovered?

Five of the eight participants said they still get emotional every now and then when they're reminded of the person who died. For three of them the feelings are still quite strong. One boy whose loss happened a year ago said: 'I still get very emotional, yes.' One girl who lost a very close relative five years ago said that she sometimes still cries when she's alone.

Q10   How would you describe death to someone who hadn't experienced it?

Half of the people spoke about going on to somewhere else after death. They only thought of death as the end of life in this world. And they thought people were going somewhere better. One person described it as like sleep. Two people thought about it from the point of view of those who loved the person who died. 'Death is something that could take your loved ones away,' one boy said. But thinking about the way in which some people are dying, he also said death can be a relief.

Discussion

I found this research project an interesting subject to look at as it has many different points where there are themes or a big difference in the answers. The first stage of the findings that surprised me was on my questionnaire. The results were really eye opening. 99% of children have experienced either a relative or a pet die before the age of 12. From the questionnaire I found out 79% have had both one or more relatives and pets die. This shows how important it is we understand how it affects children.

When I looked at the answers from the interview a lot of the answers were the same. The eight children I interviewed all talked about their sadness when the death occurred. One thing that intrigued me was the difference in how long people grieved as it ranged from one month to five years. But it seemed that this did not depend on how close they were to the person or pet who had died. It all depended on the type of person they are. So one person could be as upset by losing their dog as another person who lost their grandparent.

Another theme was that over half the people I interviewed told me it made them appreciate life a lot more and want to live it to the full. The majority felt that it had changed them as a person in one way or another. Not everyone thought that the death taught them anything. Some did but what they learned was different. Which again indicates that your experience of death is dependent on you as an individual.

It was strange that the only people the children asked for comfort from was their family. Everybody said that it was their family and especially their mum and dad that helped them through this emotional time in their life. I would have expected children would really get support from their friends, especially as it seems everyone goes through it.

If I had more time I would have interviewed more people to get a better feeling of how death affects children. But I did find interviewing people was a lot more useful than just letting them write their answers themselves.

Conclusion

I set out to find out 'How are children affected by death and how does it change them, and change their behaviour?' What I have discovered is death affects children in all sorts of ways but when it affects their behaviour it is usually in a positive way. From my own experience of death I recovered in about six months. That was the time it took before I stopped getting upset. I went to my family instead of my friends for support. I think it was because I just didn't think about going to my friends and maybe other children are the same. It changed me in a way that I wanted to be kinder to the people I love. If I had more time I would like to do more research into whether experiencing death might make some people bully other children as they need a way to express themselves and their hurt.

Girls Want to Play too! Investigating the Views of 9–11-year-old Pupils about Mixed Gender Football

(by Ben Davies and Selena Ryan-Vig, Year 6)

Introduction

We wanted to base our research project on men's and women's football because it is a subject that we are both particularly interested in. Direct comparisons between women's and men's football show huge differences between the two. Men's football is one of the richest and most publicised sports in the world. It has been speculated that David Beckham of Real Madrid earns an average wage of £120,000 a week (http://www.football-transfers.info/squads/playerprofile.asp?playerID=371), whereas Mia Hamm, one of the best female footballers in the world earns approximately £714 a week which equals roughly £40,000 a year (Match Magazine, October 2003, Edition 442). We calculated that David Beckham is earning three times as much in a week as Mia Hamm does in a year.

During a two month period of observation we found that male football was televised on average eight times a week whereas a women's game wasn't shown at all. We also looked through a set of twenty papers and calculated that there were over forty reports on male football matches in one month, taking up three to five pages a day. In the same month we found four small reports with no photos on women's football, and this was during their world cup. Women's football isn't even considered as a sport by some people, and, even though women's football is an international sport it has only been recognised as this by the Olympic Committee and FIFA, the world football governing body, since 1990. Men's football has been recognised as a sport since 1880 (www.fifa.com).

Would women footballers be more equal with men footballers if mixed gender football was played at an adult level? Currently girls and boys can play football together up until the age of eleven. After this they have to play in single gender teams only. The website run by the Football Association says the *'physical differences between the average secondary school boy and girl mean that the way they play the game begins to change too. Boys' football involves more long passing and crossing, while girls' football tends to feature more dribbling and short passing'* (www.thefa.com).

Interestingly on the same website we found an article saying that Italian Serie A male side Perugia have signed Swedish midfielder Hannah Ljunberg for £12m from an all female team. The gender rule has not been enforced in Italy allowing Perugia to sign the female midfielder and play her in their otherwise all-male first team squad. At the time of writing she has already scored 1 goal. (www.thefa.com)

Clearly not everyone thinks women and men should not play together. We think that mixed gender football is very popular and wanted to find out what other people our age thought about it. We both started off doing different projects, but we thought that it would make the projects more interesting to have male and female views. It also helps that both of us play for local football teams and at school. Our research question was: What are the views of girls and boys on mixed gender football?

Methodology

We decided to use a multi methods approach to answering our research question. We thought this would allow us to answer the question in the most thorough way possible. The different methods are outlined below.

1.   Questionnaire to the whole class

We thought about the area that was the most important for our particular interest and believed it would be the GENERAL OPINION of people our age towards mixed gender football. This was the base to our whole project.

In the questionnaire we used everyday informal language as we thought that this would help the participants to feel more relaxed. If anyone found it hard to understand we were there to help explain. The questionnaire contained closed statements, with four boxes to choose an answer from –strongly agree, agree, disagree and strongly disagree. To help with consistency in the responses we typed each question twice, once positively and once negatively.

We thought about pupils who might have difficulty reading the questions and decided that we'd help them with reading because we did not want to exclude anybody. We didn't find it very hard to make the questionnaire ethical because it's not a particularly sensitive subject though we still went out with only ethical intentions, trying not to include any upsetting questions.

We didn't ask for the participants' names as we felt this may have caused us to judge their answers. We didn't ask for their age because we knew everyone was either 9 or 10 and believed that this would have no impact at all. We did ask for gender though as this was very important and gender was the whole focus.

We gave the questionnaires out in school time with special permission from our teacher. We firstly explained to the children what we were doing and summarised our whole project for them so that they knew what to expect from the questionnaire. We then gave the questionnaires out and each person had 10 minutes to fill it in. We were glad to see that the majority was interested in our project, and we believe that this made the children concentrate just that little bit extra.

2.   Experiment

We decided to organise a selection of mixed gender football games as well as a single gender game (boys versus girls). We asked permission of our teacher, head teacher and PA/PE teacher and decided to ask 10 boys and 10 girls to volunteer. We split them up evenly into 4 teams of 5. The teams did not have a set pattern. (E.g. 2 girls on one team with 3 boys then 3 girls on one team with 2 boys.) We just picked the names out of a hat to make up the teams. All games were 5 minutes each way and were played either in the morning or afternoon away from the other children who were in their playtime.

Unfortunately there were a couple of confounding variables which may have had an overall affect on the results that we received. Firstly, we had to change the pitch from the pavement to grass. The weather also set us off course for a few days as well. If any of the players were sick we were unable to postpone any matches. We did not want to do this anyway as it might have affected the other players' enthusiasm.

3.   Observations

To observe the pupils playing football we had a clipboard, pen and paper, and moved around the outside of the field noting everything down we observed about the style of play and the attitudes to the game. We went out with open minds ready for everything and did not interrupt the game at all.

There were two main observers and also spectators who often commented on the style of play and gave their opinions on how they felt towards mixed gender football. These comments were very valuable contributions to our conclusion.

We looked mainly at the attitude of the players and we could see from that how they felt towards mixed gender football and one sex football. The style of play was probably the most important issue though, bringing out the players feelings towards mixed gender football.

After the games we took our observations and notes and wrote them out. We picked out the fine details and drew the conclusions by comparing each other's observations and combining this with the information we had obtained. We always compared each others work fairly and we were never biased in favour of our own gender or friends. We also took into consideration that we really had to reach out for girls to play, while the boys said yes straight away.

4.   Players' Questionnaires

We designed the players' questionnaire in a simple format, choosing a simple style of language suitable for all abilities and basing it on the general knowledge of each individual. We made the questions self-explanatory so that the players would not have to waste time trying to figure out what everything meant.

We used various techniques in the questions to find the information we needed from the children. We wouldn't have been able to make such an effective questionnaire if we didn't know the participants as well as we do. We made the questionnaire enjoyable and as informal as possible.

We used a number of different styles of questions. Some of the questions were open but occasionally we received closed answers. For two of the questions we used attitude scales, both on a scale of one to ten, whilst for two other questions we used yes/no techniques. However, for these questions we also received open answers.

We designed the questions so that the children would not feel pressured, upset or embarrassed and all participants were able to remain anonymous. We explained to everyone what we were doing and what we wanted to find out. We didn't ask for age because we knew that they were all nine or ten and we thought that this gap would make no difference to the results. We did ask for gender in a simple tick box.

We gave out twenty questionnaires and received twenty back. We gave them out all in one go and gave the participants fifteen minutes to complete them.

5. Captains' Interviews

We decided to interview the captains of the teams after the mixed gender matches had been played. We knew that this would be a perfect opportunity to gather as much information as possible on their feelings towards the matches. We made the questions quite personal but designed it to be confidential. We wanted the captains to pick out particular people and mention various aspects of their game, with their strengths and weaknesses. We wanted the questions to be quite hard which they may not have been able to answer straight away.

We thought of the interviewees and their kind of learning level, and thought that they all seemed to be at roughly the same achievement area. We thought of the appropriate vocabulary and questions to use. We used straight-forward questions and if they didn't understand a word or statement we always rephrased it or used a simpler more understandable word/phrase. We used mostly open questions so that they could tell us how they felt. Other questions were a mixture of open and closed, but we mostly received open answers.

While designing the interviews we thought to ourselves: is this right for us to ask them to open up their personal views? We also thought about whether to interview all of the participants or just these select few. In the end we only interviewed the captains who were all boys. A limitation to our interviews was that we only used this technique towards boys and were therefore unable to get a mixed gender opinion.

The interviewees were able to remain anonymous as we thought this would be the fairest way for them to give us more confidential detail. We asked the four captains if they wanted to be interviewed and straight away they all said yes. We knew their gender but asked them their age. We took the children into our medical room one by one so no one else could hear the answers they were giving. This was done one day after the experiment and one of us had a pen and paper whilst the other was the interviewer. We asked them all the same questions.

We explained what we were doing to all of the participants and also everything they needed to know about what we were trying to find out and the general idea of our project.

The Findings

Class Questionnaire

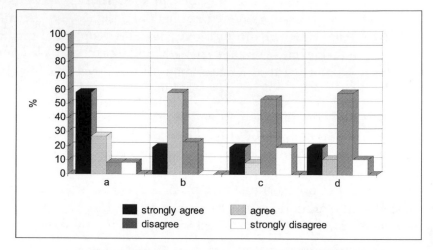

A = there should be mixed men and women's premier football league
B = mixed male and female teams are better than all male or all female teams
C = male only teams are better than mixed or female only teams
D = female only teams are better than mixed or male only teams

Figure 13.2 Responses to questions 1, 2, 3 and 4 on the class questionnaire

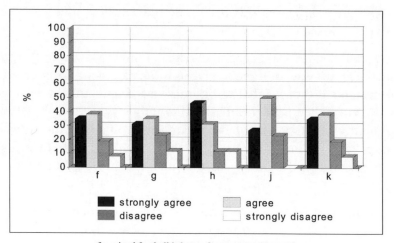

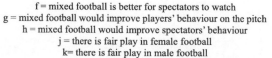

f = mixed football is better for spectators to watch
g = mixed football would improve players' behaviour on the pitch
h = mixed football would improve spectators' behaviour
j = there is fair play in female football
k= there is fair play in male football

Figure 13.3 Responses to questions 5, 6, 7, 8 and 9 on the class questionnaire

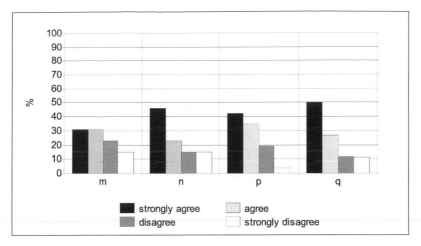

m = I think football is too obsessed with money
n = I think football would be more enjoyable for everyone if males and females played together
p = I think mixed football would encourage people to be more social
q = there is fairer play in mixed football

Figure 13.4   Responses to questions 10, 11, 12 and 13 on the class questionnaire

Observations

Boys	Girls	Overall
• Boys involved the girls more than we expected • Boys were less rough with girls than they would have been with the boys • Boys passed the ball more when they were with there own sex • Boys weren't as rushed in mixed gender football as they were in single sex football	• Girls joined in more than usual • They were more dedicated to the games than boys • They weren't afraid to tackle • They weren't afraid to argue with the ref	• The boys helped the girls get into the game • It was a better game than a single gender game • You could see that they weren't as physical • Everyone seemed to enjoy mixed gender football more than single gender • Girls and boys worked together as a team

Figure 13.5   Observations made during the mixed gender football matches

Players Questionnaire (see Analysis section)

Captain interviews

Person	Did you enjoy playing in the joint matches?	How do you think your team played?	Would you play again in a joint match?	Do you think the referee was strict?	How do you think the referee could have been better?	Extra Question or comment
1	It was fun and we worked as a team	We worked very hard against 3 hard teams	Yes if we kept these teams, if we changed the teams we would have to work very hard	Not argue with an adult ref., but maybe argue with a child ref.	Ref. couldn't be better, very good for age	**Question – If you had an older ref. would you play differently?** – No I would do fair tackles
2	Yes	Played well apart from Michael (changed name) committed lots of offences	Yes, unfair teams! Discipline 'Michael'. Or take him off 50/50 system	No! Sort of ref. I was expecting. Really good but stricter (a little). Michael needs to be disciplined	Ref. to be more experienced, but I have a good attitude	
3	Yes	I don't think I have the best team but they play well	Yes, I don't care about the teams I just want to play	Ref. not strict	Wouldn't change anything. Real ref. is too hard to take, too strict. I would do softer tackles with a child ref. Some goals should have been disallowed	**Referring to role in the game** – I had the biggest challenge
4	Yes	50/50	Yes, with the same and other teams	Not strict, but fair play, everything was fair. Decisions are fair	Ok, you couldn't improve anything	**Comment on ref** – I don't argue with the refs. decision **Comment on game** – I like the teams its challenging **Comment on player** – more tactical for Brian **Comment on player** – Bethany (changed name) should learn how to take throw ins. Tanya (changed name) shouldn't be afraid of the ball. Sue (changed name) was mucking about.

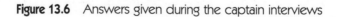

Figure 13.6 Answers given during the captain interviews

Analysis of the Findings

Class Questionnaire

Figure 13.2: We started our analysis by looking at the questionnaire that we gave to the whole class. We found that 82% of all children would like a mixed gender league, with 57% of the 82% strongly agreed to there being a mixed gender football league. 77% of children agreed that mixed male and female teams are better than all male or all female teams, whilst 23% of children disagreed. We found that 30% thought that female or mixed teams were not as good as male only teams, but 70% thought they were as good. Similarly, 70% disagreed that female only teams were better than male or mixed gender teams. These results show us that the general opinion of the class towards mixed football is positive. It is clear that a majority of children think mixed gender is better than single gender football.

The statement that produced the strongest opinions was to do with a mixed men's and women's premier league. We can't say why this statement produced the strongest opinions but it could be because the premier league is on TV and in the papers so much. We asked the people who thought that mixed gender teams were not as good as single gender teams why they thought this and they thought it might be because they had been bought up with only single gender leagues.

Figure 13.3: 73% of people agreed that mixed football is better for spectators to watch. 65% thought it would improve players' behaviour on the pitch, whilst 78% thought it would improve spectators' behaviour. 73% thought that there is fair play in women's football, whilst 69% thought there is fair play in men's football. These results again show that people's opinion of mixed gender football is positive. The majority of children believe that mixed gender football would be better to watch, and improve the behaviour of players and spectators. There was no difference in the opinions on fair play, with the majority of people believing that there is fair play in both men's and women's football.

Figure 13.4: The results from figure 3 again show the majority of people expressing positive opinions towards mixed gender football. 68% thought that football would be more enjoyable if males and females played together, whilst 77% thought that mixed gender football would encourage people to be more social. 77% of people also thought that there is fairer play in mixed football, with 50% of these strongly agreeing.

Observations

Figure 13.5: We were quite surprised at what we found in the observations that we made. The boys involved the girls a lot more than we anticipated, though they did pass it more to their gender. Three of the observations we made about the boys were to do with them changing the way they played when they played with the girls. Boys were less rough with the girls then they were with their own sex. Boys were more relaxed playing with their own gender and they passed the football about more when they were playing on the single sex team. These observations indicate that the boys are treating the mixed gender football differently to playing solely with boys.

The observations of the girls showed that they joined in more in the mixed gender football; they were also more dedicated to the match whereas some boys were messing about in the single gender game. This again indicates that the boys weren't taking the game seriously, whereas the girls were.

Overall the girls and boys worked as a team. The mixed gender football was not as physical. Also the boys helped the girls get into the games. However we thought that the boys felt that they were playing against a lower class team in the boys vs. girls single gender game. Both teams were equally willing to tackle and argue with the referee. The mixed gender games were a lot more exciting and everyone seemed to enjoy them more.

Players Questionnaire

When asked about the differences they noticed in mixed games both boys and girls gave answers that indicated the games changed (e.g. more social; not as rough; played differently together; more fun) Three of the girls compared to one boy mentioned differences between the girls and boys ability (e.g. girls good boys not; girls played better). One boy thought that the boys and girls worked together whereas no girl agreed with this. Both boys and girls agreed that the games were not as rough. All of the girls thought that they played better whereas no boy agreed with this. One boy thought that there were no differences in the mixed gender game. These answers indicate again that there were some differences between the mixed gender and single sex games in the way that they were played.

This is supported by the finding that 71% of the boys and 75% of the girls said they played differently in the joint games compared to how they would normally play when they were just with their own gender.

When asked about whether they would like to play mixed football again only 11% of boys and girls showed little interest in playing in a mixed team game again.

The majority of both boys and girls did not think that the referee was easier for either the girls or the boys.

These results from the players' questionnaire show again that there were some differences in the way that the mixed gender games were played. However, these differences don't seem to affect the enjoyment or motivation to play in a mixed game again.

Captain Interviews

Figure 13.6: All captains enjoyed the matches and would play again even though not everyone thought that the teams were fair. Nobody thought that the referee was strict. Three of the four captains thought that their teams played well, the other thought that they could have played better. These answers support the finding that the mixed gender games were as enjoyable as the single sex games and that the captains would want to play in them again.

Discussion

We are pleased with our results and we think that this was because we enjoyed this subject. From the analysis we think we have found three main findings. Firstly, the general opinion towards mixed gender football of both boys and girls is positive. We thought that it was absolutely brilliant that 82% of our class would like a mixed gender football league. Other significant results that indicated the positive opinions of children to mixed gender football are 77% of children agreeing that mixed male and female teams are better than all male or all female and 73% thought mixed football was better to watch.

The second main finding we found was that the boys and girls seemed to treat the mixed gender games differently. This is supported by our observations of the football matches in the experiment and the answers given to some of the questions on the players' questionnaire. For example 71% of the boys and 75% of the girls said they played differently in the mixed gender games.

We don't know why this is but think it could be because the boys feel that the girls are not as physically strong. More research on this would need to be done before we could definitely say why the boys and girls changed the way they played.

The third main finding was that the mixed gender games were enjoyable to play in. This finding came out in the observations, players' questionnaires and captain interviews. For example, 88% of both boys and girls gave an answer between 8 and 10 to indicate whether they would like to play in a mixed gender game again.

Conclusions

We have both enjoyed writing this report as it is a subject that we are very interested in. We think that female football would have the same universal publicity if it had been taken into consideration earlier. We both love and play football for a local team but we are both angry at F.I.F.A (Federal International Football Association) as they have refused to accept mixed gender football as a proper type of football. We are also angry at the English association who even though they are trying to increase the amount of mixed gender football leagues are not doing enough to promote it.

Therefore we decided to base our project on these subjects. Our project has turned out very well and the results we received were very interesting. They showed us that girls would love to play football with boys but they are just not able to because of the poor understanding of the original basis of football. Boys are able to find somewhere to play very easily, while girls find it a lot harder. We feel this is decreasing the real talent and potential of females.

We think that the physical differences aren't as big as people make out. In men's football there is a whole range of physical differences and we think some women would be as strong as some of the men. Further research on the exact differences is needed. If there are some women who are as strong as men playing in the premiership, shouldn't they be allowed to play? We hope that our project will help to highlight these issues to the football community.

There have always been males commanding football who only let males into their teams, they think that females are not as physically strong and as good, however most male and female players have equal ability. We do not understand why the football association refuses to change the norm. We hope that in the future projects like this one will help change the minds of the leading minds in football.

'Hey, I'm Nine not Six!' A Small-scale Investigation of Looking Younger than your Age at School
(by Anna Carlini and Emma Barry, Year 5)

Introduction

We were interested in this subject because there was somebody in our class, Kaz, who looked much younger than her age and we wondered how this affected her. We are both average size for our age and so it's hard for us to imagine what it must be like for Kaz. Also, we had noticed that other children responded differently to her, particularly in the playground. There were other children in the school who also looked a lot younger than their age and we thought this would be an interesting topic to research. We decided to investigate this but knew that we could only do this on a small scale so we decided to focus on just two pupils, one in our class, Kaz, aged 9, and another in a different Year 5 class, Rose, aged 10 (their names have been changed for this report). In our opinion they both looked about six years old. We approached both girls and explained to them what we wanted to investigate and asked whether they would be willing for us to observe them for a few weeks and then interview them. They both agreed.

Methodology

We used two methods to collect our data, observation and interview. During break times and lunch times we observed Kaz for a period of one whole week and made notes into a Dictaphone as we watched. We then did the same for Rose during a second week. Then we interviewed each of them and taped the interviews. We used a semi-structured interview technique in that we had some set questions we wanted to ask both of them but also wanted them to be able to respond freely so that we could pick up on things as they answered.

The Findings

Observations

From our Dictaphone observation notes we looked at things that kept happening each day and started grouping these together, into 'themes' of the way other children responded to them in the playground.

Kaz

Theme 1: Being treated like a cuddly doll

- Her friends kept picking her up (Kaz seemed to like this)
- Her friends kept swinging and twirling Kaz around (holding Kaz around her middle)
- Kaz was being hugged quite a lot (no-one else in the group was being hugged)

Theme 2: Trying hard to get attention

- Kaz kept hanging onto people in her group
- Kaz kept gripping onto friends' hands and arms
- Kaz often shouted loudly and if nobody took any notice she shouted louder and louder. She was shouting the loudest in the group.

Theme 3: Actions linked to her small size

- Kaz was often crouching down low to the ground
- Kaz was ducking
- Kaz was hanging onto friends from behind (almost hiding behind them)
- If Kaz got 'caught' in the tag game she yelled more often (and more loudly) than the others to get free and usually friends came straight away to get her free –more quickly than any of the others

Rose

Theme 1: Being treated like a cuddly doll

- Rose got picked up quite a lot
- Rose got twirled round a lot
- Friends were playing at trying to 'stretch' Rose

Theme 2: Trying hard to get attention

- Rose kept clinging onto people
- Rose tried to pull people away to get their attention
- Rose kept hanging onto people's arms and pulling them
- Rose was yelling a lot louder than anyone else in the group

Theme 3: Actions linked to her small size

- When playing tag, Rose didn't get chased as much as the others
- If Rose tried to 'take charge' most ignored her
- If another person in the group started talking when Rose was talking the others ignored Rose and started to listen to the new person
- Rose kept running off and nobody bothered about her and I think nobody noticed that she had run off –this might have been because she was so much smaller
- Rose kept 'ducking' a lot

Interviews

In the semi-structured interviews we asked some core questions to both girls.

- How old are you?
- How old do people usually mistake you for?
- Does looking younger than your age upset you?
- Are there any good things about looking really younger than you are?
- Are there any bad things about looking really younger than you are?
- Does looking younger than you are affect your friendships?

- Do you ever get bullied because of your size?

We also asked some questions from our observation notes such as whether they liked being picked up and swung round and about them shouting louder than the other children did. Both girls said they thought they looked about six. Kaz didn't seem to be particularly upset by this and saw more advantages than disadvantages:

'when I go to the fish and chip shop I get lollipops'.

But Rose did seem bothered by this. She could only think of one advantage – being able to play with toys where older children were usually banned, like crèches –but said there were loads of disadvantages:

Rose: Once somebody mistook my sister for being older than me and my sister said yes.

Interviewer: How old were you at the time?

Rose: Eight.

Interviewer: And how old was your sister?

Rose: Six.

Interviewer: How did it make you feel?

Rose: Angry! Well you'd be angry if your little sister laughed at you.

Interviewer: Was your little sister bigger than you?

Rose: Only a couple of centimetres.

Neither of them thought that this affected their friendships because their friends liked them for who they are not how big they are. Both of them had been bullied by girls a lot taller than them. In Kaz's case this was by girls of her own age and in Rose's case this was by girls who were two years younger (although still taller than her). The bullying happened when they were both seven but has not happened again since then. When we asked them about being swung round a lot in the playground they both said they liked this but that they didn't like being picked up as this felt like being 'babied'.

Conclusions

Even though we only observed and interviewed two girls we found out quite a lot of things and also some things that we hadn't expected to find out. There were some things that were the same that we noticed especially the way other children responded to them in the playground, in treating them sort of like dolls because of their small size. Kaz and Rose seemed to like the nice parts of this like being swung round but not being picked up and babied. There were also similarities in the way both girls needed to yell loudly to get attention. We think this might be because of their small size and that they find it harder to get people to notice them. Although lots of other children who aren't small for their age get bullied what was interesting was that Rose got bullied by children who were two years younger than her and this must hurt even more and perhaps make you less able to tell anyone about it because you feel embarrassed that it's someone younger than you doing the bullying.

We weren't very experienced researchers when we started doing this and if we could do it all over again we think we would do it better because we would be better at interviewing and ask more open questions that give us more information. Also if we were to do it again we would need to do this with larger numbers and with boys as well, so that we could see if there were any similarities between boys and across both boys and girls. Even though this is only a small project we still think there are some interesting things that it has uncovered that could be followed up with other children who are also very small for their age:

- Do they get picked up and swung round a lot by other children?
- Do they get bullied by younger children?
- Do they have strategies for getting noticed like shouting loudly?
- Do they feel there are more advantages than disadvantages in looking younger?

We have been wondering whether adult researchers would have found out what we did if they had investigated this topic. We think they would have been more experienced at interviewing but on the other hand Rose and Kaz might not have told them as much as they were prepared to tell us because we are the same age as them –for instance Rose might not have told an adult about being bullied by someone younger. Also because we are used to the kinds of games that our age play at break times we can more easily see if something is different or unusual. We hope to be able to return to this topic and investigate it more widely in the future.

Photocopiable Resource Bank

All these photocopiable resources are available to download from the PCP website: http://www.paulchapmanpublishing.co.uk/resources/kellett.pdf

▶ **Read the following newspaper report and then write about whether you consider it to be valid research. Some think prompts are given.**

UK Fast food diet producing 'fat' babies

New statistics out this month suggest that our obsession with fast food is now producing fat babies. This year a record number of babies – 103 – have weighed in at more than 12lb 12 oz. According to figures from the Office for National Statistics, 1.68% of babies weighed more than 10lb this year compared with 1.45% ten years ago. Boy babies weigh an average of 7lb 8oz, a rise of 2oz from 1973. Experts state that babies who are padded with fat all over their bodies – including, in some cases, their skulls – have a greater tendency to become obese. In Japan where fast food is not as popular and the average diet includes an abundance of raw fish the average birth weight is 6lb 10oz and in India the average birth weight is less than 6lb.

Think prompts:

■ Is this report 'research'?

■ Would you describe it as systematic, sceptical and ethical?

■ What other information would a researcher need before she or he could draw the same conclusions as this journalist?

■ How differently do you think a research report might be constructed?

_____

_____

_____

_____

_____

_____

_____

_____

_____

_____

_____

_____

_____

How to Develop Children as Researchers © Mary Kellett, 2005

Record-keeping Index: **Record No** ......

Author(s) (surname(s) plus initials)

....

....

Year of publication ....

Title...

....

Publisher ....

Thumbnail summary ....

....

Key point 1 (page)..

Key point 2 (page)..

Good quotation I might use (page   ) ....

....

Record-keeping Index: **Record No** ....

Author(s) (surname(s) plus initials) ....

Year of publication ....

Title...

....

Publisher ....

Thumbnail summary ....

....

Key point 1 (page)..

Key point 2 (page)..

Good quotation I might use (page   ) ....

....

....

How to Develop Children as Researchers © Mary Kellett, 2005

The ethical dilemma

An 11-year-old boy, Joséf, is dying from a very rare form of cancer. There is no known cure and he only has a few months left to live. Researchers are in the process of developing a new drug which they think may be able to cure this cancer in the future if it could be caught at an early enough stage. The drug is not perfected yet and even if it were, Joséf's cancer is already far too advanced for it to be able to cure him. However, doctors could learn a lot more about the drug and its potential if they could test it out on Joséf. Although this would not help Joséf it could benefit many more children in the future. There is a possibility that there might be some side effects from the drug but the doctors cannot be sure as it has not been tested on humans before. Joséf's parents are against this and are refusing to give their consent. They want Joséf to have the best possible quality of life and to be left in peace for the few months he has left. But Joséf would like to help the doctors and says he wants to do some good with his life before he dies. Who should have the final say on consent? Should Joséf, aged eleven, be allowed to overrule his parents or should his parents wishes prevail? Who else might influence the decision-making process?

Role play character parts

Joséf Wants to have the drug and insists it's his body and his life.

Mother Wants Joséf to be left in peace so that the family can make the most of the little time they have left together.

Father Angry that the doctors should have approached them with this proposal, says this is emotional blackmail and that Joséf is being exploited.

Sister Supports Joséf.

Doctor Arguing for the possible benefits for other children.

Nurse Undecided.

Additional roles for larger numbers – younger sibling, grandparent(s), second nurse.

How to Develop Children as Researchers © Mary Kellett, 2005

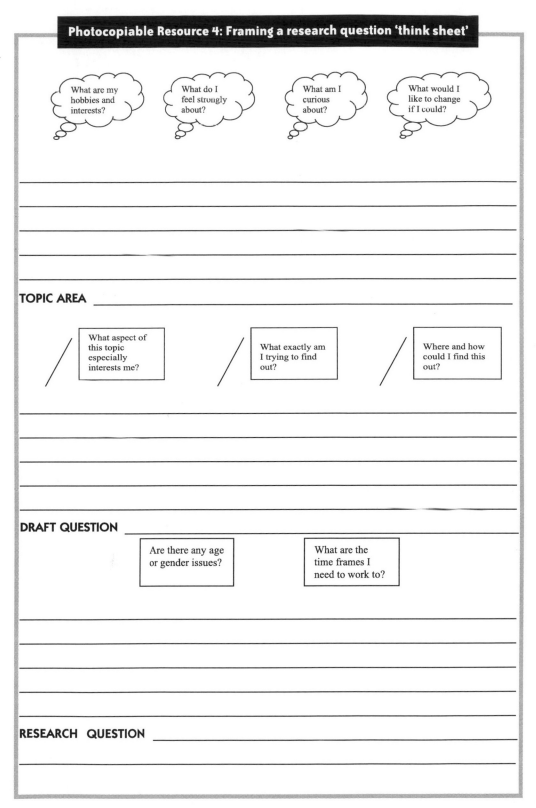

What are my hobbies and interests?

What do I feel strongly about?

What am I curious about?

What would I like to change if I could?

TOPIC AREA _____

What aspect of this topic especially interests me?

What exactly am I trying to find out?

Where and how could I find this out?

DRAFT QUESTION _____

Are there any age or gender issues?

What are the time frames I need to work to?

RESEARCH QUESTION _____

How to Develop Children as Researchers © Mary Kellett, 2005

EXTRACT 1 – FROM JADE'S OBSERVATION NOTES

Bretby School, Class 7G, Observation of Manzoor during Geography lesson, Wednesday 21st January 2004 10.20am

… It's been drizzling with rain all day so far and it looks like it will be wet break again. I'm sitting here waiting for the supply teacher to arrive. Mrs Jackson, our Geography teacher has been off ill all week – or so we're told!! – so I don't know who we'll be getting today. The teacher arrives. It's a lady supply teacher, quite old. Manzoor looks up to see who's come in. Manzoor starts to listen. The teacher asks a question and Manzoor looks around to see who's putting up their hand. Manzoor digs around in his pocket and pulls out his mobile phone. He puts it under the table where the teacher can't see it and starts to text. He is listening to the teacher again now. Manzoor is reading from his text book … Dean's just asked me if he can borrow my gel pen, I told him not to bother me when I'm doing important observing for my research …

EXTRACT 2 – FROM JACK'S OBSERVATION NOTES

Bretby School, Class 7G, Observing Manzoor (Geography lesson), Wednesday 21st Jan 04 10.20am
Teacher arrives – supply
Manzoor looks up, nudges Paul next to him, nods towards Teacher and whispers something
Manzoor starts to listen
Teacher asks Manzoor a question, M looks around to see who's putting up their hand
Manzoor chewing pencil
M starts doodling
M gets out mobile phone under the table & starts texting
M begins to listen again
M turns round to chat to Ali
M realises he should be reading something from his text book
M asks P what page it is
M finds page and starts to read
Reads (about 2 mins)
Looks up to see what T is doing (handing out worksheets)
T asks him what he's doing out of his seat 'just dropped me pencil Miss' (smirking)
Sits down again, laughing and looking round to see which of his mates are watching him
Reads a bit more …

How to Develop Children as Researchers © Mary Kellett, 2005

EXTRACT 3 –FROM INDRA'S OBSERVATION NOTES

Manzoor (Geog) 21/01/04 – 10.20am

ST arrives
M looks up, nudges P next 2 him, nods 2 T & whispers 'another old fossil'
M starts 2 listen
T asks a ? M looks ↻ 2 C whos puttg up hands
M chewg pencil
      doodlg
      lookg ↻
      gets out mobile under table & starts textg
      begins 2 listen again
      turns ↻ 2 chat 2 A
      realises should b readg somethg from text bk
      asks P what page it is
      finds page and starts 2 read
      reads – ↺ 2 min
      looks up 2 C what T doing (handg out worksheets)
      pulls face, flicks pencil on floor, gets up 2 pick it up
T asks him what hes doing out of seat
M – 'just dropped me pencil Miss' (smirkg)
      sits down again, laughg & lookg ↻ 2 C which of his mates are watchg him
      reads a bit more
      turns ↻ to chat to A again (A is fillg in his worksheet and wont respond)
      ....

Interviewer:	Hi Rashid, thanks for coming along this morning to talk to me.
Rashid:	That's okay.
Interviewer:	I understand that you have recently finished doing SATs at your school.
Rashid:	Yeah.
Interviewer:	How long did that last for?
Rashid:	The whole week.
Interviewer:	Were there many tests?
Rashid:	About two each day.
Interviewer:	And how long did the tests last for?
Rashid:	Some were 45 minutes but they changed.
Interviewer:	Did you get very tired?
Rashid:	Yeah, all the way through.
Interviewer:	More tired at the end of the week?
Rashid:	Yeah.
Interviewer:	How difficult did you find the tests?
Rashid:	Most of the tests were quite hard, because we hadn't gone on to those subjects in the whole year, in Year 6.
Interviewer:	Which of the tests did you find the easiest?
Rashid:	The easiest one was the English long task – I enjoyed that.
Interviewer:	And which was the hardest?
Rashid:	The maths first calculator.
Interviewer:	And when will you find out the results of these tests?
Rashid:	June, quite late in June.
Interviewer:	What do you think about having the tests marked by an external examiner and not by your own teachers?
Rashid:	Well, it will be kind of strange because they might not be able to know what you've written if you've kind of rushed it or something.
Interviewer:	Did you get worried at all, before the tests?
Rashid:	Yeah before the test, it was quite off-putting when you're writing them.
Interviewer:	Was that just before the tests, or you got worried the night before?
Rashid:	It was like most of the week before you got quite nervous.
Interviewer:	Do you think you were able to do your best on the day?
Rashid:	Yeah, some of the tests I could have done better, because I didn't finish them but most of them I did well.
Interviewer:	And do your teachers help you to practise for the SATs in the weeks leading up to them?
Rashid:	Yeah, cos we did like mock SATs which help you answer the type of questions that you'll be given.
Interviewer:	And how much lesson time does that take up?
Rashid:	Usually it's a whole lesson would be doing tests, just to learn how to do them.
Interviewer:	Do you think there is too much testing at school?
Rashid:	Sometimes it feels like there's too many tests, but I guess it is all for your benefit.
Interviewer:	Which of these words do you think would best describe SATs? Okay, fun, stressful or hateful?
Rashid:	Okay.
Interviewer:	And if there was a choice between sitting SATS or having your teacher just assess your work what would you prefer?
Rashid:	Assess your work.
Interviewer:	Thank you very much Rashid that was really interesting. Thanks for coming along.

How to Develop Children as Researchers © Mary Kellett, 2005

Interviewer:	Hi Emma
Emma:	Hi
Interviewer::	Thanks very much for coming along this morning to talk to me. I understand that you have recently finished doing the SATs at your school.
Emma:	Yes
Interviewer:	Can you explain to me what that was like?
Emma:	It was OK and it was sort of fun, because we got to like do no work in the afternoons, but it was hard with all the revision when you got home.
Interviewer:	So you didn't have to do any tests in the afternoon, you just did tests in the morning.
Emma:	Yes, just tests in the morning, then we just did games and PE and stuff in the afternoon.
Interviewer:	And then you had free time?
Emma:	Yes
Interviewer:	That was nice. Do you normally have much games time in class time or is that special?
Emma:	We only get about 2 hours a week. But we had like 3 hours last week which was fun.
Interviewer:	Can you describe to me some of the emotions you felt before you were doing the SATs and the time leading up to the SATs?
Emma:	I kept on feeling like, because I'm not good at certain subjects, I kept on feeling, quite like upset and like, I wasn't exactly upset but I sort of felt a bit nervous, and like I might run out of time and I might not do them well enough. But when I was running up to the ones I was good at like science I didn't feel nervous and I really wanted to get in and do them, and I found them quite fun.
Interviewer:	You enjoyed the science ones the most, which tests did you feel most nervous about?
Emma:	Spelling and mental maths
Interviewer:	Spelling and mental arithmetic. How does the mental arithmetic go? What do you have to do that makes you nervous?
Emma:	I'm scared that I won't have enough time and it will go onto the next question.
Interviewer:	I see so they ask a question and you have to answer within a set time?
Emma:	Yes, on the tape.
Interviewer:	It's on the tape, do you find that particularly stressful?
Emma:	Yes a bit because it's like you don't know sort of when they're going to start and sometimes you can't really understand them.
Interviewer:	So do you get much time to practise doing that sort of thing or …
Emma:	We do it every week on Friday. So I did practise it quite a lot.
Interviewer:	What sort of other things you do to prepare for the SATs in school in the classroom?
Emma:	We like make posters and revise that sort of way and we also just do mock SATs tests and stuff, but we do like at the beginning of maths, we also do a SATs question.
Interviewer:	Do you think there is too much testing in schools?
Emma:	Well, I don't think there is because testing doesn't really affect you so you can't really have too much of it but sometimes I think there is because like for three or four weeks you just get tested you don't actually learn anything.
Interviewer:	What about them being marked by external examiners what do you think about that Emma?
Emma:	Sometimes I find that strange, cos what happens if they can't read my writing and what if they don't understand what I mean? Cos my teachers know I can't write really well.
Interviewer:	So when you do a piece of work and your teacher's going to mark it you feel that she will understand much more what you were trying to say?
Emma:	Yeah, 'cos my teachers are used to how I write.
Interviewer:	So if you had a choice would you rather your assessment was done by your teacher than by someone external?
Emma:	Yeah.
Interviewer:	So what would your friends think about that – or is that something that you think.
Emma:	I don't know if my friends would think the same but they probably would because they also like … they don't like the wait for it to be sent off and back again.
Interviewer:	Have you got any brothers or sisters who are doing SATs?
Emma:	Yeah, my brother's in Year 9 and he did his SATs.
Interviewer:	How did he find the SATs?
Emma:	He found his quite stressful because it affected his GCSEs.
Interviewer:	Right. So what's the atmosphere like at home when it's SATs time?
Emma:	It's sort of really edgy because everybody's really stressed and they get angry all the time.
Interviewer:	Well thank you very much for coming along to talk to me this morning Emma, I found that really interesting.

How to Develop Children as Researchers © Mary Kellett, 2005

Interviewer:	Hi Jamie, thanks very much for coming along to talk to me this morning.
Jamie:	Okay, thank you for your time as well.
Interviewer:	What's it like being in Year 6.
Jamie:	It's better than being in Year 5 because when I came in Year 5 I didn't know anyone and was pretty afraid cos I didn't know anyone and I didn't know what anyone was like. But it's a lot better now cos I know all my friends. It's okay I suppose. I'm not that sure. I'm okay it's just sometimes I have a falling out with my friends quite a lot and that's basically it and then just have fun and games and then I'm fine really.
Interviewer:	What's different about being in Year 6 from any other year?
Jamie:	It's got a lot harder with SATs. The questions are really hard. I worked a lot harder to get my level four and it's just been great to know that I have done really well.
Interviewer:	You mentioned SATs – I'm not sure what SATs are – can you explain a little bit about what they are?
Jamie:	It's basically an exam and it's trying to get you in to for next year what classes and what level you are at – so there's level one, level two, level three, level four. It's pretty hard I suppose but you get through it. It's not as hard as what you think really, it's a lot easier.
Interviewer:	What do the levels mean Jamie?
Jamie:	Level four means that you are working at level 6 like Year 6. Level 3 is around five and four, then three is 3 and 4, 2 is around 2 and 3 and 1 I don't think they have any exams cause it's a bit too hard for them.
Interviewer:	How do you feel about being given a level?
Jamie:	I feel fine actually, as long as I know that I've tried my best and just good to know I've done it cos I've worked hard for it.
Interviewer:	And the level that you're given, somebody external decides that, do they, from the test, they're externally marked?
Jamie:	I don't know really, I'm not sure.
Interviewer:	What do you think about how the level should be decided, what's your opinion?
Jamie:	My opinion most probably would be that as long as everyone tries their best that they should get the level they want and that's it really.
Interviewer:	The tests that you have to do for these levels, do they last a long time?
Jamie:	No there's a forty-five-minute one, twenty-minute one another forty-five minute one in English and then the science is just forty-five minutes for both of the SATs papers and maths is basically the same.
Interviewer:	So you only have tests in English, maths and science? Anything else?
Jamie:	No.
Interviewer:	What do you feel about that?
Jamie:	I'm not really bothered. I'm glad that there's only three cos then it'll just be more harder. It'll just take longer to do and you'll get more shaken up.
Interviewer:	With more and more tests in more and more subjects. Supposing there weren't any tests and you just had your teacher give you a progress report at the end of year instead – what would you think about that?
Jamie:	I would most probably feel okay I suppose – not really bothered just as long as I know that it's just been a good day to do it.
Interviewer:	Does it ever affect friendships – is there ever any rivalry?
Jamie:	There might be. There was one time but it went down then after a little while.
Interviewer:	And what about at home?
Jamie:	My mum just makes me try my best and she's not really bothered as long as I try my best and I get where I want to go.
Interviewer:	Do you have to do these SATs at any other time, have you done any before?
Jamie:	You have to practise all through the year – there's just the one that you get your levels on.
Interviewer:	All through the year so you've being practising at the beginning of the year?
Jamie:	There is one SATs test every term I think just to test you to see how far you are and how much you need to go to get to where you want to be.
Interviewer:	Does that take up a lot of class time?
Jamie:	I suppose so, yeah, it takes up about 2 hours of the day.

How to Develop Children as Researchers © Mary Kellett, 2005

Interviewer:	And is that time you think you would rather be doing something else or are you quite happy?
Jamie:	Quite happy, trying to practise to get so that I know that I can get further if I need to.
Interviewer:	When do you start thinking about SATs? Do you think about it when you're in Year 5, Year 4…?
Jamie:	I don't really think about it, just try and take it easy. When it comes to it do my best.
Interviewer:	And when do you find out your results Jamie?
Jamie:	I think it's the end of next term, 'cause we have just finished them about a week ago I think it is, a week or two, and they come back like a month later, because they have to be checked by a few different people just to make sure that they are all the right marks.
Interviewer:	A long time to wait do you feel?
Jamie:	I'm not really bothered I'm glad I don't get them really soon back 'cause then I'd just be worried about them but sometimes I do worry about them 'cause they take so long and then I think that I've done wrong so it all depends really.
Interviewer:	What form does the worrying take?
Jamie:	Just don't really want to go to school nothing like that 'cause I'm worrying so much about it.
Interviewer:	Does that happen a lot Jamie?
Jamie:	No, it only happens when SATs comes, just get really scared.
Interviewer:	Do many of your friends get scared?
Jamie:	Yeah, quite a lot of them do.
Interviewer:	What do you do when you get scared to try and get through that?
Jamie:	Usually just sit down and think about it by myself and then think how I'm going to do it and just remind myself and that I have to try my hardest for myself and not for anyone else.
Interviewer:	So you don't go and tell anyone you feel scared?
Jamie:	No.
Interviewer:	You wouldn't tell your mum or your teacher, or another friend?
Jamie:	No.
Interviewer:	Are you glad they're all over now?
Jamie:	Yeah – a lot gladder.
Interviewer:	Well, I wish you the very best of luck when you get your results. I'm sure you've done really well.
Jamie:	Thank you.
Interviewer:	Thanks very much for coming to talk to me this morning.
Jamie:	Okay.

How to Develop Children as Researchers © Mary Kellett, 2005

Questionnaire 1

	Agree	Disagree
1. School uniform is a good idea		
2. I hate wearing school uniform		
3. Teachers should have to wear a teacher uniform		
4. Children should be able to choose whether they wear school uniform or not		
5. Children should only wear school uniform from Year 3 upwards		
6. School uniform should be banned		

Questionnaire 2

	Agree	Neither agree nor disagree	Disagree
1. School uniform is a good idea			
2. I hate wearing school uniform			
3. Teachers should have to wear a teacher uniform			
4. Children should be able to choose whether they wear school uniform or not			
5. Children should only wear school uniform from Year 3 upwards			
6. School uniform should be banned			

How to Develop Children as Researchers © Mary Kellett, 2005

Questionnaire 3

	Strongly agree	Agree	Neither agree nor disagree	Disagree	Strongly disagree
1. School uniform is a good idea					
2. I hate wearing school uniform					
3. Teachers should have to wear a teacher uniform					
4. Children should be able to choose whether they wear school uniform or not					
5. Children should only wear school uniform from Year 3 upwards					
6. School uniform should be banned					

Questionnaire 4

	Strongly agree	Agree	Slightly agree	Neither agree nor disagree	Slightly disagree	Disagree	Strongly disagree
1. School uniform is a good idea							
2. I hate wearing school uniform							
3. Teachers should have to wear a teacher uniform							
4. Children should be able to choose whether they wear school uniform or not							
5. Children should only wear school uniform from Year 3 upwards							
6. School uniform should be banned							

How to Develop Children as Researchers © Mary Kellett, 2005

Scenario 1: The water drinking experiment

A researcher wants to find out whether drinking water throughout the school day improves pupils' concentration.

Task: Identify the independent, dependent and extraneous variables. Discuss what the researcher needs to do to set up a valid experiment and then consider what the ethical implications are.

The independent variable is ....

....

The dependent variable is ....

....

....

The extraneous variables are ....

....

....

....

....

....

....

....

The ethical considerations are ....

....

....

....

....

....

....

....

How to Develop Children as Researchers © Mary Kellett, 2005

Scenario 2: The human growth drug experiment

Someone has developed what they believe to be the equivalent of a 'miracle fertilizer' for human beings (rather than tomato plants!). She or he hypothesises that taking this drug will increase human growth. This could have some major benefits for individuals who have stunted growth but how might a researcher go about testing this? What are the ethical implications?

Task: Identify the independent, dependent and extraneous variables. Discuss what the researcher needs to do to set up a valid experiment and then consider what the ethical implications are.

The independent variable is ....
....
....

The dependent variable is..
....
....

The extraneous variables are ....
....
....
....
....
....
....

The ethical considerations are ....
....
....
....
....
....
....

How to Develop Children as Researchers © Mary Kellett, 2005

Scenario 3: The baby colour preference experiment

A researcher wants to investigate whether 9-month-old babies show any strong colour preferences, and if so whether this is different for girls and boys. She has a play pen, three coloured teddies (brown; pink; and blue) and a stop watch.

Task: Identify the independent, dependent and extraneous variables. Discuss what the researcher needs to do to set up a valid experiment and then consider what the ethical implications are.

The independent variable is ....
....
....

The dependent variable is ....
....
....

The extraneous variables are ....
....
....
....
....
....
....

The ethical considerations are ....
....
....
....
....
....
....

Transcript extract 1: Observations of Kaz first break Mon 2nd December

… She's yelling louder than the others.

She's crouching down,

She's yelling more.

Yelling more loudly than the others.

Yelling even louder.

She's crouching down again.

Kaz is hanging onto people,

She's gripping onto them.

Yelling loudly again.

Still yelling loudly.

More yelling loudly.

More loudly than the others.

More loud yelling.

She's being picked up and carried like a baby by one of the group.

Someone else has picked her up now.

Someone else has picked her up and is rocking her.

They are holding her by her middle and swinging her around.

Kaz is hanging onto people.

The group are playing tag. Every time Kaz tries to run someone catches her.

Kaz is gripping onto them, hanging on their arm.

She is still gripping onto them.

Kaz has to stand still because she's caught.

She's yelling more loudly than the others to get free. The others aren't yelling to be got free.

Someone has come straight away to get her free.

Kaz is being hugged now.

More hugging.

More hugging.

No-one else in the group is being hugged.

No-one else in the group has been hugged for the whole of break time …

How to Develop Children as Researchers © Mary Kellett, 2005

Transcript extract 2: Observation of Rose first break Thursday 5th Dec

… She's being picked up.

She's being twirled round and then put down again.

They're choosing who is going to be 'tug' and 'it', Rose is trying to take charge.

Some are doing what she says but most are ignoring her.

Someone else has started to speak and they're listening to the new person and ignoring Rose.

Rose isn't getting chased as much as the others in the tag game.

Most of the time she's just staying on her own.

She keeps running off and nobody is bothering about her.

Now she's gone up to someone in the group and she's clinging, gripping on to them, sort of hanging on really.

Bending forwards and running.

Ducking, sort of thing.

Screaming and shouting loudly.

Ducking a lot more.

Now she's got her arm round some of her friends.

Yelling loudly.

Being picked up again.

Being 'stretched'.

More 'stretching'.

Picked up again.

Someone else has picked her up now and is walking round with her – she's put her down now.

She's being hugged and patted …

How to Develop Children as Researchers © Mary Kellett, 2005

Table 10.3 Number of passes (excluding goal keepers) expressed as percentages

Football match	SCHOOL A {girls n = 5; boys n = 5}				SCHOOL B {girls n – 5, boys n = 5}			
	Passes by boys to boys	Passes by boys to girls	Total number of passes	% passes boys to girls*	Passes by boys to boys	Passes by boys to girls	Total number of passes	% passes boys to girls*
1	31	9	40	23	49	5	54	9
2	26	20	46	44	37	3	40	8
3	17	16	33	49	39	4	43	9
4	38	5	43	12	60	8	68	12
5	19	17	36	47	51	8	59	14
6	32	10	42	24	42	6	48	13
7	43	29	72	40	43	9	52	17
8	27	11	38	30	48	9	57	16
9	25	16	41	39	66	10	76	13
10	21	12	33	36	42	7	49	14
Totals	279	145	424	34 {average % from the 10 matches}	477	69	546	13 {average % from the 10 matches}

* rounded to the nearest whole per cent

▶ **Scrutinise the data provided in Table 10.3 and write about or discuss what you can deduce from the data. Think about the following:**

■ Is a valid comparison being made between the two sets of data?

■ What conclusions can you draw?

■ These data only relate to two schools. Is this enough to be able to make any generalisations about mixed gender football?

How to Develop Children as Researchers © Mary Kellett, 2005

Set of data relating to pre- and post-test scores after an experimental spelling teaching approach was used for half a term

Participant	Pre-test spelling score (%)	Post-test spelling score (%)
A	48	68
B	32	62
C	87	88
D	76	79
E	52	63
F	12	53
G	92	92
H	60	68
I	18	60
J	69	74

▶ Scrutinise the data in the table above and write about what you notice from your analysis. Do you notice any patterns or trends? What conclusions might you draw?

_____

_____

_____

_____

_____

_____

_____

_____

_____

_____

_____

_____

_____

How to Develop Children as Researchers © Mary Kellett, 2005

Introduction –about 200 words (more if you are including a review of literature)

In this section write about:

- What you were interested in and why.
- What you wanted to find out.
- What other people have already found out (if anything)
- Finish this section by stating what your research question(s) is(are).

Methodology –about 500 words

In this section write about:

- Whom you did your research with and how you decided on your sample
- How you went about finding data to answer your research question(s). This means describing in detail each of the methods you used.
- The time scales of your study.
- All the ethical considerations for your study and what steps you took to consider the ethical sensitivity of what you were doing (e.g. making questionnaires anonymous; considering children who might have difficulties with reading; thinking about children's feelings etc.)

Findings –graphs and/or tables or descriptive findings

This is the section where you present your results. Quantitative data are best presented in graphs and/or tables and qualitative data in an organised compilation of the descriptive findings.

Discussion –about 500 words

In this section write about what you found out from your results and your interpretations of your findings. As you do this also write about how this affects any wider considerations e.g. if you are doing some research on bullying and your results show that a lot more boys are bullied than girls, what are the implications of this?

Conclusion –about 200 words

In this section write about what conclusions you can draw and what other research might be possible from the first steps you have made.

References

Include a list of references for any work you have cited.

Appendices

These sometimes contain tables of 'raw data'; blank questionnaires; interview transcripts.

How to Develop Children as Researchers © Mary Kellett, 2005

My research was about the opinions of Year 6s at my school about the use of computers in lesson time now don't think 'research how boring,' because it's not. I am really excited by computers and find them so interesting you can make a computer do almost anything except make it take your dog for a walk! Think about some of the wonderful things computers have done for us they design cars, they make films like 'Basil the Great Mouse Detective' and they make it possible to produce CDs. Now they even tell streetlights when to turn on! I wanted to find out how much pupils enjoy using computers in their lessons at school and whether they thought they got enough computer time in some different subjects like Geography and English not just about Maths and Science. I decided the best way of collecting my data was to do a survey so I designed a questionnaire. I included a 'don't know category' because I wanted to be sure that the pupils did really agree or disagree and added the strongly categories to find out if there was any strong feeling about any of the statements. I thought of the kind of statements I would need that would help me get the right kind of data. I used a five-point agreement scale: strongly agree; agree; don't know; *disagree and strongly disagree.* This was to give the pupils plenty of choice so that they didn't feel pushed into answering yes or no. I made the questionnaire anonymous except for ticking whether they were a girl or a boy because I was also interested to see if there were any gender differences. The questionnaire had eight statements. I enjoy using computers at school. I like XP computers better than window 98. Computers should be easier to use. Everybody should have their own personal laptops for lessons. Computers should be lowered in price. I want to use computers more in English. I want to use computers more in Geography. I want to use computers more in Maths. The replies came back over about three days and only three from the class did not return them. First of all, I separated the replies into girls and boys. Because I was interested in how much computers were used in lessons and whether there were enough computers I thought it would be useful to interview a teacher to get an adult view about computers The numbers of boys and girls in the class are not exactly even so I turned the responses into percentages to make it easier to compare the two groups. I used a calculator to do this and rounded the percentages to the first decimal point. This is just a small study but it would be interesting to do it with lots more classes to see if the results were the same and to follow up the questionnaire with some interviews of boys and girls to find out more exactly what some of the gender differences might be. The majority of children from both genders enjoy using computers. NO children dislike using computers, although a few girls and boys ticked the 'don't know' box. There are a few more boys who strongly like using computers but no significant difference is made. It seems that no children are afraid of using computers so perhaps they could be used more often. No pupils disliked the XP computers more than the 98s. Though no girls 'strongly' liked the XPs, all 100% of the girls agreed with liking the XPs more than the 98s. Should there be a new range of computers each year? But what about the expense? There was a fairly even spread of opinion about computers being easy to use and no real gender differences. Does this mean that computers are already easy to use at the moment or is it just that pupils are getting much better at using them? That's something I could try and find out if I do any follow up work. I think the question about laptops is a bit futuristic because I doubt the schools would provide children with their own laptops but it was interesting to see what pupils thought all the same. Girls were slightly more in favour of this than boys but as you can see nearly everybody would like to have their own laptop. Although pretty much everyone thought that computers should be lowered in price, boys don't think computers should be lowered in price quite as much as the girls and there was slightly 'stronger' feeling in the responses from the girls. It was in the opinions about how often to use computers in these three different subject lessons where the greatest gender differences were. Girls disagree with using computers more in English than boys, but boys have most percentage on the strongly agree. I wonder if this is because English is the subject where we write the most and perhaps girls don't find the handwriting as much of a chore as the boys. It was almost the same picture for Geography although not quite as strong. There was less difference in the genders about using computers more in Maths. Over half of both genders agreed with more computer use in Maths lessons but again it was the boys who expressed the 'stronger' feelings. I had expected that this percentage would have been higher. To me it seems like computers were practically invented for Maths – they can even work out where something would land like a space ship or guiding a plane from a to b. From this research I can see that all children, of both genders like using computers at school and find them easy to use. The majority of children would like to use computers more in school, although there were some slight gender differences here. Of the three subjects I surveyed, boys wanted additional computer time in English the most, whereas less than half of girls wanted more computer use in English. There was less strength of feeling about more computer time in Maths and Geography was about in the middle. I wonder if this is because computers are used quite a bit in Maths already but not perhaps as much in English. If children want to use computers more in class there would have to be a lot more computers around, as well as those in the IT room. Perhaps we could have an experiment for a year when one class has personal laptops that they can use whenever they want, in any lesson. We could interview them and their teachers afterwards to find out whether it made learning better.

How to Develop Children as Researchers © Mary Kellett, 2005

abstracting: a process of identifying common themes between and across sets of data.

closed question: a question which restricts the responses that can be made by having a pre-determined set of possible answers.

coding (in qualitative research): attributing codes to data in order to reduce the data mass into manageable and thematic categories.

data: information (which can be numerical or descriptive) which are analysed and used as the basis for making decisions in research. Data is plural, the singular form is *datum* but it is unusual to only ever have one piece of information in research so the word datum rarely appears in research writing.

dependent variable: the variable which shows the effect of an influence.

empirical: relates to something in our practical experience, derived from observation or experiment. It is linked to the idea that true knowledge is to be found within our practical experience rather than from speculative notions or ideas.

ethical: making sure that the well-being, interests and concerns of those involved in research are looked after. It is imperative that research does not cause harm or distress to any of the participants at any time. These days research is generally expected to follow a code of ethics laid down by an authoritative body.

ethnography: the description of a culture or a way of life through a process of 'immersion' as a participant observer in that cultural world.

focus group interview: a group interview with a focused theme where interpersonal dynamics and the interaction of participants in respect of one another's comments forms an important element in the data.

independent variable: the variable which exerts an influence.

Likert scale: a five-point scale used to measure responses in a range such as 'very good/good/neutral/poor/very poor'.

memoing: making immediate notes, throughout the initial stages of the analysis process, about aspects of the data, theory or research design that occurs to the researcher.

naturalistic: an approach that focuses on exploring the nature of things rather than testing hypotheses about them, on understanding and interpreting the world in terms of the people in that world. The world can only be understood by people who are part of that world and enquiry is consequently coloured by their individual experiences.

naturalistic observation: the observer does nothing to manipulate or stimulate the behaviour of the individuals being observed, aiming for as natural and typical a situation as possible.

open question: a question which does not limit the response that can be given nor suggest the kind of answer a researcher might be looking for.

participant observation: observation undertaken by a researcher who is also part of the action being observed, usually, but not always, associated with a qualitative approach.

population sample: a group of people who participate in research, the choice of people can be predetermined or random according to what is appropriate for the research question. The number of the population sample similarly varies according to the research question. Generally, quantitative methods have the larger population samples.

positivist: a scientific approach concerned with cause and effect, objectivity and controllability and with the ability to predict and measure. Knowledge about the world is generated by understanding these causal links.

qualitative: an approach which gathers data in a non-numerical (descriptive) form.

quantitative: an approach which gathers data in a quantifiable (numerical) form.

reflexive: a process of reflecting on the researcher's own position in relation to the action being investigated and the impact this might have on the collection of data and the analysis of findings.

sceptical: being prepared to question or doubt the nature of findings – even the most commonplace. The process of doubting is an important stage in research if we are to acquire relative certainty (we can never have absolute certainty). So, a sceptical approach tries to find things out but also looks for counter arguments which might reject as well as confirm the findings. Furthermore, researchers allow their findings to be scrutinized by other people and expect them to try and disprove the findings.

semi-structured interview: an interview based on a core of key questions with the additional flexibility of following up responses with further, more individualised questions.

statistical significance: is a measure of whether the differences of the effect showing in the data are bigger or smaller than the differences which might be expected to have happened by chance.

structured interview: a tightly framed interview consisting of a series of closed questions which are repeated in exactly the same way to all interviewees.

systematic: researchers think about what they are going to do and how and why they are doing it in a methodical, purposeful, step-by-step way. Everything is set out very explicitly, e.g. if a researcher is going to 'find out' by observation then exactly what is to be observed, who is doing the observing, how, where, in what circumstances and for how long, has to be made clear.

systematic observation: a meticulous method in which the minutiae of behaviour is targeted for observation and measured via a coding system.

triangulation: a process which uses more than one method of data collection in order to increase the validity of the research data.

unstructured interview: an interview with no predetermined questions based more loosely on conversational-style questions around the general topic area.

variable: something which can have two or more levels of difference, e.g. gender can be one of two variables – male or female – and hair colour can be one of several variables.

How to Develop Children as Researchers © Mary Kellett, 2005

REFERENCES

Alderson, P. (2000) Children as researchers, in P. Christensen and A. James (eds), *Research with Children: Perspectives and Practices*, London: RoutledgeFalmer, pp. 241-257.

Alderson, P. and Morrow, V. (2004) *Ethics, Social Research and Consulting with Children and Young People*, Barkingside: Barnado's.

Baxter, L., Hughes, C. and Tight, M. (2001) *How to Research* (2nd edn), Buckingham: Open University Press.

Borg, W.R. (1963) *Educational Research: An Introduction*, London: Longman.

Boyden, J. and Ennew, J. (eds) (1997) *Children in Focus: A Manual for Participatory Research with Children*, Stockholm: Radda Barnen.

Christensen, P. and James, A. (eds) (2001) *Research with Children: Perspectives and Practices*, London: RoutledgeFalmer.

Christensen, P. and Prout, A. (2002) Working with ethical symmetry in social research with children, *Childhood*, 9(4): 477-497.

Clark, A. and Moss, P. (2001) *Listening to Young Children: The Mosaic Approach*, London: National Children's Bureau.

Coates, E. (2000) 'I forgot the sky!': children's stories contained within their drawings, *International Journal of Early Years*, 10(1): 21-35.

Cohen, L., Manion, L. and Morrison, K. (2000) *Research Methods in Education* (5th edn), London: RoutledgeFalmer.

Elsey, S. (2004) Children's experience of public space, *Children & Society*, 18(2): 155-164.

Fielding, M. (2004) Transformative approaches to student voice: theoretical underpinnings, recalcitrant realities, *British Educational Research Journal*, 30(2): 295-311.

Frankfort-Nachmias, C. and Nachmias, D. (1992) *Research Methods in the Social Sciences*, London: Edward Arnold.

Fraser, S., Lewis, V., Ding, S., Kellett, M., Robinson, C. (2004) (eds) *Doing Research with Children and Young People*, London: Sage in association with OUP.

Gillick v. *West Norfolk and Wisbech Area Health Authority* (1985) http://www.lawcampus.butterworths.com/student/Lev3/weblinked_books/fortin/dataitem.asp?ID=12595&tid=7 (last accessed 22 August 2004).

Glaser, B.G. and Strauss, A.L. (1967) *The Discovery of Grounded Theory*, Chicago: Aldane.

Howarth, R. (1997) *If We Don't Play Now, When Can We?* London: Hopscotch Asian Women's Centre.

Johnson, V., Ivan-Smith, E., Gordon, G., Pridmore, P. and Scott, P. (eds) (1998) *Stepping Forward: Children and Young People; Participation in the Development Process*, London: Intermediate Technology Publication.

Jones, A., Jeyasingham, D. and Rajasooriya, S. (2002) *Invisible Families: The Strengths and Needs of Black Families in which Young People Have Caring Responsibilities*, Bristol: Policy Press and Joseph Rowntree Foundation.

Kellett, M. and Nind, M. (2001) Ethics in quasi-experimental research on people with severe learning disabilities: dilemmas and compromises, *British Journal of Learning Disabilities*, 29, 51-55.

Kellett, M., Forrest, R., Dent, N. and Ward, S. (2004) Just teach us the skills, we'll do the rest: empowering ten-year-olds as active researchers, *Children & Society*, published online 5th February DOI: 10.1062/Chi.807.

Kerlinger, F.N. (1986) *Foundations of Behavioural Research* (3rd edn) New York: Rinehart & Winston.

Konstant, T. (2000) Speed Reading, London: Hodder & Stoughton.

Lawrence, D. (1988) *Enhancing Self Esteem in the Classroom*, London: Paul Chapman Publishing.

Leonard, M. (2002) Working on your doorstep: child newspaper deliverers in Belfast, *Childhood*, 9(2): 190-204.

Lewis, A. (2002) Accessing, through research interviews, the views of children with difficulties in learning, *Support for Learning*, 17(3): 110-115.

Lewis, V., Kellett, M., Robinson, C. Fraser, S. and Ding, S. (eds) (2004) *The Reality of Research with Children and Young People*, London: Sage in association with OUP.

Likert, R. (1932) *A Technique for the Measurement of Attitudes*, New York: Columbia University Press.

Mason, J. (2002) *Qualitative Researching* (2nd edn), London: Sage.

Mayall, B. (2000) Conversations with children: working with generational issues, in P. Christensen and A. James (eds), *Research with Children: Perspectives and Practices*, London: RoutledgeFalmer, pp. 120-135.

Morrow, V. and Richards, M. (1996) The ethics of social research with children: an overview, *Children & Society*, 10(2): 90-105.

Nieuwenhuys, O. (2001) By the sweat of their brow? Street children, NGOs and children's rights in Addis Ababa, *Africa*, 71(4): 539-557.

Pickett, W. (2004) Multiple risk behaviour and injury: an international analysis of young people, in V. Lewis et al., (eds), *The Reality of Research with Children and Young People*, London: Sage in association with OUP.

Pollard, A. and Bourne, J. (1994) *Teaching and Learning in the Primary Classroom*, London: Cassell.

Pyke, N. (1993) Ablest 'being hindered', *Times Educational Supplement*, 22 October: 7.

Robson, C. (2002) *Real World Research* (2nd edn), Oxford: Blackwell.

Scott, J. (2000) Children as respondents: the challenge for quantitative methods, in P. Christensen and A. James (eds), *Research with Children: Perspectives and Practices*, London: RoutledgeFalmer, pp. 98-117.

Strauss, A. and Corbin, J. (eds) (1997) *Grounded Theory in Practice*, Thousand Oaks, CA: Sage.

Thorne, B. (1993) *Gender Play: Girls and Boys in School*, New Brunswick, NJ. Rutgers University Press.

Tuckman, B.W. (1972) *Conducting Educational Research*, New York: Harcourt Brace Jovanovich.

United Nations (1989) *Convention of the Rights of the Child*, New York: United Nations.

Wilson, N. and McLean, S. (1994) *Questionnaire Design: A Practical Introduction*, Newton Abbey, Co. Antrim: University of Ulster Press.

Woodhead, M. (1999) Combatting child labour: listen to what the children say, *Childhood*, 6(1): 27-49. abstraction 101-2

*I*ndex